Philadelphia Liberty Trail

Philadelphia Liberty Trail

Trace the Path of American History

FIRST EDITION

Larissa and Michael Milne

Guilford, Connecticut

An imprint of Rowman & Littlefield

Distributed by NATIONAL BOOK NETWORK

Copyright © 2015 by Rowman & Littlefield

All photographs by the authors unless otherwise noted.
Kite icon licensed by Shutterstock.com.
Maps by Melissa Baker © Rowman & Littlefield.

British Library Cataloguing-in-Publication Information available

Library of Congress Cataloging-in-Publication Data available

ISBN 978-1-4930-0157-6 (paperback)

∞™ The paper used in this publication meets the minimum requirements
of American National Standard for Information Sciences—Permanence of
Paper for Printed Library Materials, ANSI/NISO Z39.48-1992.

**All the information in this guidebook is subject to change. We recommend
that you call ahead to obtain current information before traveling.**

Dedicated to our parents, who encouraged us to see the world

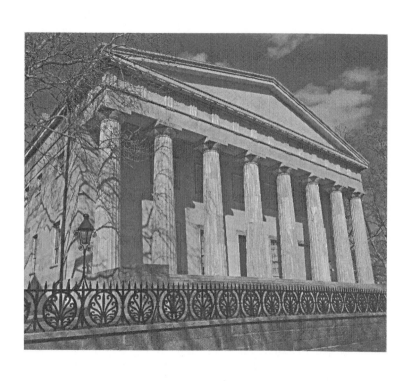

Contents

About the Authors

In 2011, Philadelphia natives Larissa and Michael Milne sold their home, quit their jobs, and gave away their possessions to travel around the world for a year with a Rocky statue. After learning to live much more simply they have continued their nomadic lifestyle with no fixed address. They focus on historical, offbeat, and tasty tales. Their stories appear regularly in the *Philadelphia Inquirer, AAA, Huffington Post,* and other media outlets. Their travel blog at ChangesInLongitude.com won the 2013 Lowell Thomas Travel Journalism Silver Award for Best Travel Blog, awarded by the Society of American Travel Writers Foundation. Despite visiting 60 countries and all 50 states, their heart still belongs in their hometown of Philadelphia, where they lived a few blocks from Independence Hall and the Liberty Bell.

Acknowledgments

We'd like to thank Philippa Chaplin of the *Philadelphia Inquirer* who first provided an opportunity to two budding travel writers; Paula Fuchsberg who made that chance possible; Adam Duncan of Independence National Historical Park; Visit Philadelphia; Philadelphia Convention & Visitors Bureau; Sheraton Philadelphia Society Hill and Wyndham Philadelphia Historic District; Del Conner at the Physick House; Al Harris at the Powel House; Stacey Peeples at Pennsylvania Hospital; Dr. Marla Miller of the University of Massachusetts for her insight into the life of Betsy Ross; Libby Browne at St. Peter's Church; George Thomas of the University of Pennsylvania; Chef Walter Staib and Molly Yun of City Tavern; John Price Wetherill, who visited from 1844 to provide us with local color at the Free Quaker Meeting House; Kelly Murphy at the Philadelphia History Museum; Ronn Shaffer of Old Pine Street Presbyterian Church; John Hopkins at Christ Church Burial Ground; Neil Ronk at Christ Church; Mark Kehres and Lauren Saul at the National Constitution Center; Alberto Gonzales at Fireman's Hall Museum; Heather Kinkade of Historic Philadelphia, Inc.; Janice Telstar; Jerry Milne; Charlie Davidson; Donald Smith; Karen Page; Larry Schroepfer, Esq.; Andy Murdock; Luca, Sofia, Kate, and Caroline for helping us view the Philadelphia Liberty Trail through the eyes of a child; the wonderful team at Globe Pequot including Tracee Williams, Lauren Brancato, and Joanna Beyer; the truly remarkable people of 17th-, 18th- and 19th-century Philadelphia whose accomplishments, large and small, made this city such an inspiring place to visit; and to William Penn for making it all possible.

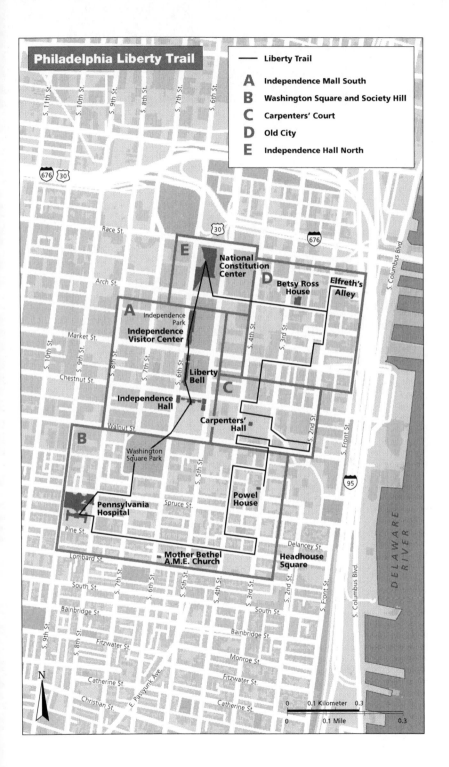

Introduction

There is an abundance of sights related to early American history in Philadelphia. Although the area surrounding Independence Hall has been dubbed "the most historic square mile in America," the attractions related to the dramatic founding of the nation have not been presented before as a unified group. This book guides you through the **Philadelphia Liberty Trail,** over 25 sights related to the birth of the United States of America.

The book is broken down into chapters that divide the historic district into five easy-to-navigate sections. Independence Mall is at the center with each section forming a rough loop that begins and ends nearby. Though the entire trail is about 4 miles long, you're never far from the starting point. Begin wherever you like; it's not necessary to follow the trail sections in sequence to get a handle on things.

Each section will take about two to four hours, depending on how deeply you like to explore. We've included **Side Trips** along the way that may be of interest, as well as **Pit Stops** for dining, shopping, or just sitting down to rest weary feet. If you're traveling with youngsters, keep an eye out for the **kite icon** 🪁, indicating kid-friendly destinations.

The back of the book contains practical travel information such as lodging and dining options along with historic sights to visit elsewhere in Philadelphia and the surrounding region.

Much of the trail meanders through Independence Park where you can pop your head into many attractions, like the Liberty Bell, for free. For others there is a small admission fee. Details are listed with each individual location.

More than half of the Philadelphia Liberty Trail takes you outside the confines of Independence Park and onto the streets of Philadelphia, giving you a peek into the world that formed a backdrop to early American history. It's where a diverse group of immigrants to 18th-century

Philadelphia—both voluntary and involuntary—made significant contributions to the cause of liberty.

Some of the sights such as Christ Church, Pennsylvania Hospital (the nation's first), Headhouse Square Market, and Mother Bethel African Methodist Church (another first) are still in operation today fulfilling their original mission. Others, such as the Powel House and Carpenters' Hall, are some of the finest remaining examples of early American building design and part of the largest collection of Georgian architecture in the world outside of London.

Explore the cobblestoned streets, majestic buildings, and tree-lined colonial neighborhoods in the city where this country began, and trace the path of American history.

Welcome to Philadelphia

> The city of London, tho' handsomer than Paris, is not as handsome as Philadelphia.
>
> —*Thomas Jefferson, 1786*

Philadelphia is more than a backdrop for quaint colonial buildings like Independence Hall and Betsy Ross's house; it's not just a place where the Liberty Bell cracked the first time it tolled. Philadelphia is where representatives came together from 13 separate colonies, men with varying goals and ideas for the future of the country. It's where in 1776 they declared their independence from Great Britain and, after they were victorious in war, reconvened 11 years later to determine what form the United States of America would take. By creating the United States Constitution they set a new world standard for representative government.

Perhaps that's because Philadelphia was a revolutionary town from its inception. William Penn welcomed people of all faiths when he created the colony in 1681 with a guiding principle of religious freedom,

what he called his "Holy Experiment." Penn was also cutting-edge in laying out the city on an efficient grid pattern, rather than the serpentine streets and alleys of old European cities that had developed organically over time.

Philadelphia grew rapidly upon the tidy framework of Penn's plan. By 1776 it was one of the largest and most forward-thinking cities in the British Empire. Its sophistication attracted leading lights in science, medicine, commerce, and the arts. According to historian Neil Ronk of Christ Church, "18th-century Philadelphia had a similar vibe to California in the 1950s. Anyone who was anyone wanted to move to Philadelphia." The new land of opportunity even lured Benjamin Franklin, who abandoned his native Boston as a youth for the greener pastures of the City of Brotherly Love.

The religious freedoms that Penn granted attracted people from all over the world who brought a new vitality to the city. As the political, financial, and industrial innovation center of the Americas, it was

Washington, D.C., Wall Street, and Silicon Valley, all rolled into one compact package.

So much excitement was created in Philadelphia that in the early 1800s it was called the "Athens of America." But unlike the relics of ancient Athens, many of the buildings where history was created in Philadelphia still stand and welcome you on the Philadelphia Liberty Trail.

INDEPENDENCE MALL SOUTH

The **Independence Mall South** section of the Philadelphia Liberty Trail includes some of the most significant sights of American history, including **Independence Hall** and the **Liberty Bell.** Take time to walk even farther in the footsteps of the Founding Fathers by strolling among the buildings facing **Independence Square** that hosted the nation's capital from 1790 to 1800, including **Congress Hall** where the United States Senate and House of Representatives met and where George Washington and John Adams were inaugurated as president. In the **Great Essentials** exhibit, you'll even see the actual Declaration of Independence that was first read to the public on July 8, 1776.

The house Washington and Adams lived in, the predecessor to the White House, is long gone. But you can learn more about the complex issues surrounding their terms of office at the **President's House Site.** A few blocks away you can see where the 33-year-old Thomas Jefferson wrote the Declaration of Independence in the re-created **Declaration House.**

Begin your exploration of historic Philadelphia at the corner Market and South 5th Streets (Independence Mall East), where you'll see a granite marker that states:

> Congress shall make no law respecting an establishment of religion, or prohibiting the free exercise thereof; or abridging the freedom of speech, or of the press; or the right of the people peaceably to assemble, and to petition the Government for a redress of grievances.
>
> *—The First Amendment to the United States Constitution,*
> *15 December, 1791*

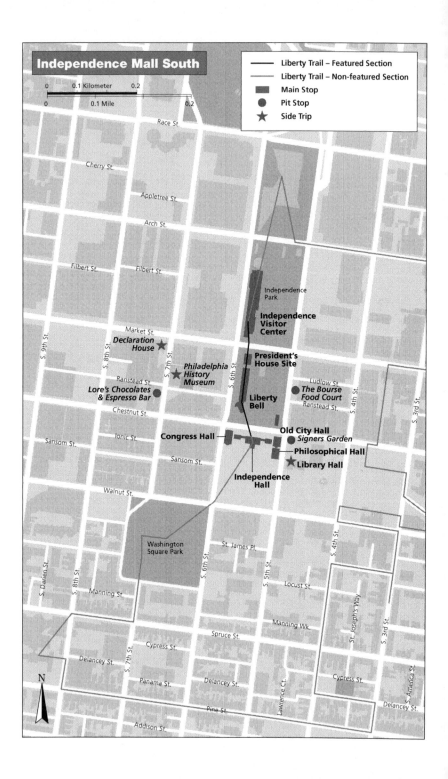

Independence Mall South

Liberty Trail – Featured Section
Liberty Trail – Non-featured Section
Main Stop
Pit Stop
Side Trip

0   0.1 Kilometer   0.2
0   0.1 Mile   0.2

Race St.

Cherry St.

Appletree St.

Arch St.

Filbert St.   Filbert St.

Independence
Park

Independence
Visitor
Center

Market St.

*Declaration
House*   President's
House Site

S. 9th St.
S. 8th St.
S. 7th St.

*Philadelphia
History
Museum*

Ranstead St.

Lore's Chocolates
& Espresso Bar

Chestnut St.

S. 6th St.

Liberty
Bell

Ludlow St.

*The Bourse
Food Court*

Ranstead St.

S. 4th St.
S. 3rd St.

Sansom St.   Ionic St.

Congress Hall

Old City Hall
Signers Garden

Sansom St.

Philosophical Hall
Library Hall

**Independence
Hall**

Washington
Square Park

S. 6th St.

St. James Pl.

S. 5th St.

S. 4th St.

Locust St.

St. Joseph's Way

S. 3rd St.

S. Darien St.
S. 8th St.

Manning St.

Manning Wk.

Spruce St.

Cypress St.

Delancey St.

S. 7th St.

Panama St.

Delancey St.

Lawrence Ct.

Cypress St.

S. America St.

Delancey St.

Pine St.

N

Addison St.

For its time this was a radical statement of rights, but it was in keeping with the profound change in government that the United States of America embraced after their victory over Great Britain. Amid a sweeping view of Independence Mall, you're standing within footsteps of where this new nation was formed to uphold these basic human rights that are literally written in stone.

Independence Visitor Center
6th and Market Streets

The best place to begin the Philadelphia Liberty Trail is at the Independence Visitor Center. It handles information requests for Independence National Historical Park as well as the city of Philadelphia and surrounding region.

Several films about Philadelphia during the struggle for independence are shown throughout the day. Visitors can pick up tickets to area

PHOTO COURTESY CHRIS ROBART

attractions, arrange tours, select from free maps and brochures, and shop in the Independence Store, the official gift shop of the Greater Philadelphia region. Aside from miniature Liberty Bells and other historic treats you can even pick up a replica Rocky statue. Amenities include 24-hour underground parking, free Wi-Fi, accessible restrooms, ATM, and a cafe.

At the Visitor Center you can also pick up free tickets to tour Independence Hall. Standing in the same room where men from 13 colonies signed the Declaration of Independence and risked "their lives, their fortunes and their sacred honor" is an essential stop on the Philadelphia Liberty Trail.

Independence Visitor Center Information

Location: 599 Market St. (Corner of 6th and Market Streets)

Hours: Daily, 8:30 a.m. to 6 p.m.; extended hours Memorial Day weekend through Labor Day weekend, 8:30 a.m. to 7 p.m.

Admission: Free

Phone: (800) 537-7676

Website: phlvisitorcenter.com/attraction/independence-visitor -center

Wheelchair accessibility: Accessible throughout

President's House Site
6th and Market Streets

During tours of Independence National Park, guides often say that the pursuit of liberty is not perfect, but it's worth preserving. These complex issues are addressed at the President's House site next to the Liberty Bell Center.

The existing structure is reminiscent of Benjamin Franklin's "Ghost House" in Franklin Court. With its random partial walls and empty

The site where Washington and Adams lived.

window frames, it reaches skyward like a Roman-ruins version of colonial architecture. Several video monitors present an exhibit called *President's House: Freedom and Slavery in the Making of a New Nation*, reenacting the lives of slaves and servants who toiled for the president. Side panels relay the story of other events that occurred in America during the administrations of Washington and Adams including the Whiskey Rebellion and passage of the Alien and Sedition Acts. The ongoing excavations of the home's foundation are viewable through glass panels.

Washington established the executive branch of government in the President's House. By definition everything he did set a precedent for future presidents, including setting up a "cabinet" of advisors and releasing an annual State of the Union report.

In its heyday the circa-1767 palatial four-story Georgian brick house was occupied by a "who's who" of early American history including **Richard Penn,** William's grandson and colonial governor of Pennsylvania; **General William Howe,** who requisitioned the home during the British occupation of Philadelphia; the notorious traitor **Benedict Arnold,** who planned his treasonous plot within these walls; and **Robert Morris,** financier of the Revolution and one of the richest men in America. When Philadelphia was the nation's capital, Presidents **George Washington** and **John Adams** each lived here during their terms of office, giving the site its current name. It's obvious it wasn't just any old house.

You Be the Judge

During Washington's residency he brought along a group of nine slaves from his Mount Vernon plantation, which caused a delicate problem for him. Pennsylvania was the first state to provide for the emancipation of slaves with the passage of the Gradual Abolition Act of 1780; if slaves lived in the state for six months they were granted their freedom. Washington got around this by a bit of subterfuge. He rotated his slaves out of Philadelphia so none of them would be there the requisite six months.

Martha Washington's personal maid was a young slave named **Oney Judge.** In 1796 the 23-year-old domestic servant left the house while the Washingtons were settled down to dinner and fled to New Hampshire by boat, seemingly safe in such a faraway locale. She set up a new life, marrying Jack Raines, a free black sailor, with whom she had three children. But due to the Fugitive Slave Act of 1793, which Washington signed into law, owners were allowed to reach into non-slave states to reclaim what was considered their property, so Judge was never truly out of danger.

In a turn of bad luck, an acquaintance of Martha Washington spied Judge in Portsmouth, New Hampshire, and reported back this information. Washington twice tried to have his wife's maid returned, but on both occasions New Hampshire officials intervened. Oney Judge Raines lived in freedom until her death in 1848, but it's hard to imagine that she didn't always have one eye looking apprehensively over her shoulder.

In an all-too-familiar refrain, despite its former grandeur and historical importance, the mansion was torn down in 1832. But it gets worse. From the 1950s until the current restoration project, the site was a public restroom, serving visitors to Independence Mall.

When the National Park Service envisioned a new Visitor's Center for Independence Park, along with an updated structure to house the Liberty Bell, there were no plans to commemorate the President's House, which was the precursor to the White House. The situation grew complicated when the history of Washington's slaves at the residence was revealed. In fact, visitors to the new Liberty Bell pavilion would be walking over the remains of the old slave quarters.

The irony of this situation was too much. The Park Service agreed to excavate the remains of the home and set up a memorial to tell the story of the slaves who lived and served in it.

A National Park Service placard states, "History is not neat. It is complicated and messy. . . . The President's House exposes the core contradiction at the founding of this nation: enshrinement of liberty and the institution of slavery." As you proceed on the Philadelphia Liberty Trail, you'll find history and events that are not always wrapped up in a pretty bow. But it's important to explore the birth of the United States of America and a notable change in how mankind was governed.

President's House Information

Location: 6th and Market Streets

Hours: Open-air pavilion that is accessible 24 hours a day. The videos run 9 a.m. to 8 p.m., daily.

Admission: Free

Phone: (215) 965-2305

Website: nps.gov/inde/historyculture/the-presidents-house.htm

Wheelchair accessibility: On a public street with access throughout

---

Liberty Bell
6th and Chestnut Streets

You have to admit, it takes a strong degree of confidence for a nation to embrace something that's broken as one of its most popular symbols. But that's the case with the cracked, but beloved, **Liberty Bell.** Over 2 million people a year visit this most famous icon of American history.

When the Liberty Bell started out it wasn't a national symbol. In fact, it wasn't even known as the Liberty Bell. It was merely a functional tool used as a colonial-era communication device. It tolled for special events both happy and sad, and called townspeople to meetings. Its symbolism came later when activities in Philadelphia had consequences reaching far beyond the sound of the bell.

In 1751 the colonists of Pennsylvania ordered a bell from Whitechapel Foundry in London. The occasion was the 50th anniversary of Penn's granting the Charter of Privileges that established the framework

Two American icons.

for the colony and granted major democratic freedoms to its inhabitants. Speaker of the Pennsylvania Assembly Isaac Norris designated that the bell be marked with a phrase from Leviticus Chapter XXV in the Bible:

> *"Proclaim Liberty throughout all the Land unto all the Inhabitants thereof."*

Abolitionists are credited with the first use of the name "Liberty Bell" in the 1830s. They embraced the bell, and the phrase on it, for their anti-slavery movement. It's been known as the Liberty Bell ever since. In an ironic twist, Isaac Norris was a slave owner.

The bell landed in Philadelphia in 1752, and although it was a year late for the 50th anniversary festivities, the colonists still excitedly greeted its arrival into the city; in an omen of things to come, it cracked the first time it was tested. (That is not the famous crack that appears today. More on that in a little bit.)

Local metal workers John Pass and John Stow were hired to fix the bell. Despite having no prior experience with bells, Pass and Stow melted the bell down and recast it, adding a bit of copper in the process. No one liked the tone of the bell, so they melted it down a second time.

In early June, 1753, this twice-reworked bell was hung in the belfry of the State House. Some wags still felt it had a "disagreeable tone" but seriously, how many times can you melt the darned thing down and

---

March Madness

Does that music playing inside the Liberty Bell pavilion sound familiar? It's the *Liberty Bell March* by John Philip Sousa, but fans of 1970s television will recognize it as the theme song of *Monty Python's Flying Circus*.

The hairline crack appears just above the manmade one.

start over? If you look closely at the bell you'll notice its rough surface, evidence that the well-meaning Pass and Stow were in a little over their heads with a project of this magnitude. But their names lived on in the inscription on the bell itself and have been viewed by millions.

The bell tolled for the next two decades, even causing some residents to complain that the ringing was a nuisance, until wood rot in the steeple made use of the 2,080-pound bell a potentially hazardous event. Accounts differ as to whether or not the bell rang on July 8th, 1776, to summon townspeople to hear the first public reading of the Declaration of Independence. It's known that bells rang throughought the city to record the momentous event, but with the State House steeple in such poor condition this bell may have been forced into silence.

Despite weighing just over a ton, the Liberty Bell has moved around quite a bit. During the late-19th and early-20th centuries, it was periodically sent around the country for various expositions. People throughout the nation often traveled hundreds of miles just to get a

Liberty Bell Information

Location: 6th and Chestnut Streets

Hours: Daily, 9 a.m. to 5 p.m. with extended summer hours. Enter through security at the northern end of the building. The Liberty Bell may also be viewed 24/7 from outside through full floor-height windows. *Note:* During busy summer hours the security screening to enter the pavilion can cause long lines. But the line moves quickly and you'll rarely wait more than 15 to 20 minutes. Once inside the pavilion you can roam around freely to view the bell.

Admission: Free

Phone: (215) 965-2305

Website: nps.gov/inde/liberty-bell-center.htm

Wheelchair accessibility: Accessible throughout the single-story pavilion

glimpse of the symbol of liberty as it passed by on a flatbed railroad car. It returned to Philadelphia for the last time in 1915, where it resided back in the familiar haunt of Independence Hall.

To allow more people to view the bell, it was moved to a small pavilion on Independence Mall in time for the Bicentennial in 1976, then on to its current home in 2003.

As you walk toward the bell you'll pass exhibits conveying the bell's history and growth as a symbol for America. Its enduring message was used most powerfully by abolitionists in the 1830s to fight slavery and later by the women's suffrage movement. The Liberty Bell itself, still suspended from its original yoke of American elm, occupies pride-of-place overlooking the building where it used to hang, Independence Hall. It's a striking tableau of two of the most powerful symbols of American history. For such a famous icon it's really incredible how close admirers can get to it.

Pit Stop: The Signers Garden

The Signers Garden is a welcoming spot to stop for a rest after touring Independence Hall and its surrounding buildings. A small park located directly opposite Old City Hall, the garden is on the site of artist Gilbert

---

Signature Events

How many of the 56 signers of the Declaration of Independence were born in the United States of America? None. The nation didn't exist at the time. (Okay, that was a trick question.) But 48 were born in the colonies that eventually became the United States. The oldest of the signers was 70-year-old Benjamin Franklin. The youngest was Edward Rutledge of South Carolina, who was only 26. As any fan of *National Treasure* knows, the last signer to die was Maryland's Charles Carroll, who passed away in 1832 at the age of 95.

The Most Valuable Autograph of the Signers Is . . .

The 56 signers of the Declaration of Independence represented a veritable "who's who" of early American history. Among them were Benjamin Franklin, John Hancock, and future presidents John Adams and Thomas Jefferson. So naturally the most valuable autograph of all the signers belongs to Georgia delegate Button Gwinnett. *Button who?* After his sojourn to Philadelphia, Gwinnett returned to his home state and in 1777 died after a duel with a political rival. Gwinnett's death at age 42 limited the availability of his signature, with only 51 known to exist. This scarcity makes his autograph the "Holy Grail" for diehard collectors trying to acquire a complete set of all the signers of the Declaration of Independence. Historical document and artifact dealers estimate a Gwinnett-signed document would fetch $600,000 today. The autograph of John Hancock, whose name has become synonymous with signatures, can be acquired for less than $10,000.

Stuart's home. Stuart is best known for his many portraits of George Washington, including one you may have in your pocket right now: Washington's likeness on the $1 bill.

The park is named for "The Signer" statue, which was donated to Independence National Park by the nonprofit Independence Hall association. Rest a bit on one of several benches that line the walkways, and you may even meet one of the park's historical reenactors who'll regale you with revolutionary tales. **The Signers Garden** is located at the southeast corner of 5th and Chestnut Streets and is always open.

Pit Stop: The Bourse Food Court and Shops

The Bourse is a mixed-use property that houses a food court and shops on the lower floors with offices above; it was built in 1895 as the nation's first commodities exchange. Today the beautifully restored Bourse retains the grandeur of an 1890s European shopping arcade.

Situated right on Independence Mall, only a block from the Liberty Bell, it's a convenient place to take a breather in the midst of the busiest historic sites.

Food options are similar to those found in shopping-mall food courts across the country: pizza, Chinese, deli, smoothies, ice cream, and more. For those looking for that perfect souvenir, several shops offer virtually anything remotely Philadelphian. You'll find that copy of the Declaration of Independence, Liberty Bell pencil sharpener, Phillies T-shirt, or even a miniature statue of Philadelphia's second-favorite son after Benjamin Franklin, movie icon Rocky Balboa.

Kids won't want to miss **Franklin's Ghost,** a free attraction on the Concourse Level, where a hologram of Philly's favorite Founding Father "chats" with visitors about his inventions, his politics, and more.

The Bourse is located at 111 S. Independence Mall East and is open from 10 a.m. to 6 p.m., Mon to Sat, year-round and from 11 a.m. to 5 p.m. on Sun between Mar and Nov.

Independence Hall
520 Chestnut Street

> We hold these truths to be self-evident, that all men are created equal, that they are endowed by their Creator with certain unalienable Rights, that among these are Life, Liberty and the pursuit of Happiness.
>
> —*Thomas Jefferson, the Declaration of Independence*

The Assembly Room in Independence Hall, where the Declaration of Independence was debated and signed, is the most historic room, in the most historic building, in the most historic square mile in America. Also known as the Signers' Room, it's the spot where some of the same men met a decade later to create the US Constitution, establishing the

Independence Hall
The State House of
Pennsylvania

The Birthplace of
the UNITED STATES
of AMERICA

There are no public restroom facilities once you pass through security to tour Independence Hall. Public restrooms are located nearby at the corner of 5th and Chestnut Streets and in the Independence Visitor Center.

framework of government for the United States. For American history buffs it doesn't get any better than this.

What we know today as Independence Hall started life as the State House of Pennsylvania in 1732, coincidentally the same year George Washington was born, with the construction continuing in fits and starts through 1748. Designed jointly by Pennsylvania Assemblyman Andrew Hamilton and builder Edmund Wooley, the grand brick building proclaimed to the world that Pennsylvania was a colony to be taken seriously.

A firsthand description of the State House on the eve of revolution comes from *The Universal Magazine and Literary Museum*, a publication edited in 1774 by Samuel L. Wharton:

> *The State House . . . is a large handsome building, two stories high. . . . To the West is a large room in which the Supreme Court is held, and another on the East, in which the Assembly meet. In the hall is a handsome staircase which leads up to the third story of the steeple . . . part of the steeple being entirely of wood is in such a ruinous condition that they are afraid to ring the bell, lest by so doing the steeple should fall down.*

The Assembly Room is decorated as it was in July 1776, when a group of delegates from the 13 colonies sweltered in the summer heat and debated the political course they would take. On July 2nd, Congress agreed to a resolution for independence, which was introduced by

The back of Independence Hall faces Chestnut Street.

Virginian Richard Henry Lee. It was a monumental step that paved the way for the events of July 4th.

John Adams felt the vote on Lee's resolution was so important that he wrote to his wife Abigail, predicting that July 2nd would be the most important day in American history, one that would be celebrated every year with "bonfires and illuminations" across the continent. He was off by two days but he did get the concept right.

Once the delegates agreed they would separate from Great Britain and the king, they spent the next two days finalizing the document that proclaimed the colonies as a united and independent country. The **Declaration of Independence** was passed in this very room on July 4, 1776. The document itself was created by 33-year-old Thomas Jefferson, with some editing along the way by members of Congress.

Contrary to popular belief, only two men signed the Declaration of Independence on July 4, 1776: John Hancock, as President of the Continental Congress, and Charles Thomson as its Secretary. This document was passed along to printer John Dunlap to create 200 copies for distribution throughout the colonies. Unfortunately the original version with the two signatures was lost.

When most people think of the Declaration of Independence it's the fading manuscript on display at the National Archives in Washington, D.C., with all 56 signatures. Known as the "engrossed" copy, it was prepared in late July 1776 by Timothy Matlack and signed by a majority of the delegates on August 2nd. The remaining signatures were collected over the next several months as the delegates made their way back to Philadelphia. The tale about John Hancock boldly penning his name in extra-large letters so even King George III could read

The most historic room in America.

it is probably not true; the signed document was never sent to Great Britain.

In 1787 the delegates of the 13 states met in this same room to craft a document determining how the emerging country would be governed. Some of the furnishings are original, including the **"Rising Sun" chair** that George Washington sat in during the proceedings that created the Constitution. Benjamin Franklin remarked that he wasn't sure if the sun carved into the chair was rising or setting, but once the Constitution was signed he happily concluded that it was a rising sun.

The silver inkwell sitting on the table is a reproduction of the one that was used to sign both the Declaration of Independence and the Constitution; the original inkwell crafted by Philip Syng is on view in the **Great Essentials exhibit** next door in the West Wing of Independence Hall.

The Supreme Court of Pennsylvania heard cases in the mustard-colored room on the western side of the first floor. While the Assembly Room opposite it is entered through a doorway so members can discuss their issues in private, the judicial chamber is wide open, reflecting William Penn's belief in open trials. Note the wooden cage where the accused "stood" trial.

Climb upstairs through the sweeping staircase in the bell tower. Along the way peer through the large Palladian window for a bird's-eye view of Independence Square. The first room on your left served as the formal Governor's Council Chamber until the state capital left for Lancaster in 1799.

The Long Room on the second floor runs the length of the building along Chestnut Street. It was originally the Banqueting Room and was the site for elegant dances and extravagant feasts. In 1802, after Philadelphia was no longer the state or federal capital, the room was transformed into a museum by Charles Willson Peale, with paintings

The Rising Sun Chair.

High style in the colonies.

and unusual scientific artifacts. Many of his depictions of 18th-century American luminaries are now found a block east in the Portrait Gallery at the Second Bank of the United States.

During their occupation of Philadelphia from September 1777 through June 1778, British troops used Independence Hall as a stable, makeshift hospital, and holding cell for American prisoners-of-war. The "redcoats" no doubt took a perverse delight in keeping American soldiers captive in the very building where independence was declared only a year earlier.

The building wasn't always as revered as it is now. In the decades after the Revolution the State House became yet another functional government building. By 1816 the state of Pennsylvania was willing to sell off the building to be razed for new development. Fortunately the city of Philadelphia stepped in and purchased it, perhaps realizing what a boon it would be for future tourism. When Lafayette toured America in 1824 a renewed interest in the Revolution blossomed, resulting in the first use of the phrase "Independence Hall" to refer to the State House and the renaming of the park it fronted "Independence Square."

Independence Hall does look a bit different today than it did during the time of the Revolutionary War. In 1829 William Strickland replaced the rotted steeple that had been removed 50 years earlier, adding clock faces that are now seen from all four sides of the tower.

Perhaps the lowest moment for Independence Hall came in the mid-19th century. In the 1850s Congress passed an updated Fugitive Slave Act, which more aggressively allowed the capture of runaway slaves anywhere in the country. For cases in Philadelphia, hearings took place in a federal courtroom on the 2nd floor of Independence Hall. The very building where a document declaring "all men are created equal" was signed was used to return men and women to captivity. In a sad counterpoint to that era of turmoil, Abraham

The appropriately named Long Room.

The rebuilt tower with clocks added.

Lincoln's body lay in state in the Assembly Room after his assassination a decade later.

Independence Hall has become such an iconic building that replicas of it can be found across America including at Knott's Berry Farm in California, where interior scenes for *National Treasure* were filmed. When actor Nicolas Cage is unfurling the Declaration of Independence in the Assembly Room and declares to his accomplices, "The last time this document was in this room was when it was signed," well, he's standing in California.

The bell that rings in Independence Hall today is the Centennial Bell, hung from the tower for the nation's Centennial in 1876. The 6-ton bell contains metal from Revolutionary and Civil War cannons. Visitors staying in the historic district will hear it peal hourly as a reminder of the freedom that was declared in Philadelphia in 1776.

Independence Square

Old City Hall/West Wing of Independence Hall/
Congress Hall

6th and Walnut Streets

Independence Square, formerly State House Square, is not one of the original squares that William Penn set aside for public parks, but it serves that function today with the memorable backdrop of Independence Hall soaring overhead. In 1760 several houses fronting Walnut Street were purchased and torn down to create permanent open space, several years before anyone could have foreseen the future historic importance of the site.

It's where on July 8, 1776, **Colonel John Nixon** of the Pennsylvania Militia first read the Declaration of Independence to the public. After the recitation, part of the crowd stormed the

The unbeatable view from Independence Square.

Supreme Court chambers in the west room of the State House and tore down the wooden coat-of-arms representing King George III. They then paraded it through the streets, before using it as fuel for a festive bonfire. (The public reading of the Declaration of Independence is reenacted annually on July 8th at high noon, although without the burning of the king's coat-of-arms.)

Several buildings face onto Independence Square: **Independence Hall** with its two outbuildings, **Philosophical Hall, Old City Hall,** and **Congress Hall.** The southern section of the square along Walnut Street is parkland with easy pedestrian access. However, to enter the historic buildings visitors must pass through the security screening area located on Chestnut Street between Old City Hall and Independence Hall. (For Independence Hall you'll need a free ticket, which is discussed in the Independence Hall section.)

Independence Hall Information

Location: 520 Chestnut St.

Hours: Daily, 9 a.m. to 5 p.m. Entry is through security booth at eastern wing of the building near 5th and Chestnut Streets.

Admission: Free, but timed tickets for the 30-minute tour are required and issued at the Visitors Center daily on a first-come, first-served basis. The National Park Service recommends showing up by 10:30 a.m. to get tickets for that day. Tickets are not required Jan and Feb or on July 4, Veteran's Day, or Thanksgiving. Tickets can also be reserved up to one year in advance (restrictions apply) through the National Park Reservation system online at recreation.gov or by phoning (877) 444-6777. For details and recommended visiting times, see the Independence National Historical Park website (listed below).

Phone: (215) 965-2305

Website: nps.gov/inde/index.htm

Wheelchair accessibility: First floor only

Old City Hall

5th and Chestnut Streets

Old City Hall is a federal-style structure that was built in 1790 for Philadelphia's municipal government. But with the nation's capital returning to Philadelphia after a seven-year hiatus, the building soon housed the Supreme Court of the United States.

After the capital moved to Washington, D.C., in 1800, the building served as part of Philadelphia's city hall and judicial complex until 1901. Today it's furnished as it looked when it housed the first Supreme Court. It probably won't be more than a 15-minute visit, unless you shop for souvenirs in the Independence Square Museum Store that takes up the remainder of the first floor. The shop is generally open from Apr through Dec.

The clip-clop of horses passing by Old City Hall.

The Supremes

During the Supreme Court's first term in Philadelphia in February 1791, the court adjourned the session after only two days because they had no cases on which to rule. President Washington nominated New York native John Jay as the first chief justice of the Supreme Court. Unlike today's lifetime tenures, Jay only served for five years. When he stepped down Washington nominated South Carolinian John Rutledge to succeed him, but the Senate failed to confirm Rutledge. Think about that when watching today's contentious Supreme Court battles—even the revered Washington couldn't get one of his choices through the arduous process.

Old City Hall Information

Address: 5th and Chestnut Streets

Hours: Daily, 9 a.m. to 5 p.m. Enter through the Independence Square security booth at 5th and Chestnut Streets.

Admission: Free

Phone: (215) 965-2305

Website: nps.gov/inde/old-city-hall.htm

Wheelchair accessibility: First floor only

West Wing of Independence Hall

520 Chestnut Street

The West Wing of Independence Hall houses the **Great Essentials Exhibit.** Other than the National Archives in Washington, this is one of the most impressive displays of artifacts anywhere related to America's founding, yet visitors often overlook it. Take a few moments to step inside and you'll be rewarded with a view of priceless original

The famous Syng inkstand.
PHOTO COURTESY CHRIS ROBART

broadsides of the documents that created America: the **Declaration of Independence,** the **Articles of Confederation,** and the **Constitution.** Displayed alongside is the silver inkstand crafted by **Philip Syng** that, according to longstanding legend, was used by the signers of the Declaration of Independence and the Constitution to wet their quills before signing those storied documents.

The actual copy of the Declaration of Independence that Colonel John Nixon read on July 8, 1776, is on display. (It was passed down through his family.) It's next to a copy of the Constitution that is the final draft printed by John Dunlap and David Claypoole. There is one final handwritten correction on it, purportedly made by George Washington, before the printers prepared the final copy and sent it via stagecoach to New York where Congress was meeting.

Worth More Than the Paper It's Printed On . . . Much More

When the Continental Congress gave formal approval to the Declaration of Independence on July 4, 1776, they sent it off to printer John Dunlap with a rush order of 200 copies. These "Dunlap broadsides" were dispatched by horseback throughout the colonies, where they were often read aloud at public gatherings. Of the Dunlap broadsides, only 26 are known to exist; the most recent was found by an American antique book dealer who was poring over a box of documents in the National Archives of Great Britain in 2008. One of them popped up in 1989 when a lucky bargain hunter bought a framed painting at a flea market in Pennsylvania Dutch Country for $4. A copy of the Dunlap broadside was tucked into the frame behind the painting. What a serendipitous discovery; he sold it to an art investor for $2.4 million who then sold it at auction in 2000 for $8.1 million to television producer Norman Lear. It's toured around the country so as many people as possible can view this American treasure. But what happened to the draft copy of the Declaration that Dunlap worked off of to make the copies, the one that Jefferson painstakingly composed and Congress revised? No one knows. Maybe it's waiting to be discovered at another flea market.

West Wing of Independence Hall Information

Address: 520 Chestnut St., attached to Independence Hall

Hours: Daily, 9 a.m. to 5 p.m. Enter through security booth at 5th and Chestnut Streets.

Admission: Free

Phone: (215) 965-2305

Website: nps.gov/inde/westwing.htm

Wheelchair accessibility: The compact exhibit is wheelchair accessible.

Congress Hall
6th and Chestnut Streets

A sterling example of federal architecture in its own right, Congress Hall often gets lost in the shadow of its illustrious neighbor, Independence Hall. But many events of historical significance transpired within the walls of the circa-1789 structure. It only operated for a short time as a county courthouse before it was handed over to the US Congress in 1790 after the capital moved here from New York.

Congress Hall was the site of **George Washington's** inauguration for his second term as president. Four years later **John Adams** was sworn in here. Adams's inauguration was a significant moment in world history, representing a peaceful transfer of power, a concept practically unheard of for revolutionary leaders. When King George III was told that Washington would voluntarily relinquish his power as head of the Continental Army when the war ended he said, "If he does that, he will be the greatest man in the world." Well, he stepped down then and he stepped down again at the end of his presidency. Both times he just wanted to return to his home at Mount Vernon.

The Life of the Party

Although George Washington's second term as president did not end until 1797, he published his **Farewell Address** in a Philadelphia newspaper, the *American Daily Advertiser*, in September 1796. It was his way of notifying the American public that he would not seek a third term and would return to private life. His parting thoughts included: warnings against entering permanent alliances with other nations; a criticism of forming political parties that can "become potent engines by which cunning, ambitious and unprincipled men will be enabled to subvert the power of the people, and to usurp for themselves the reins of government"; and that virtue and morality were necessary for the proper functioning of government.

The seat of federal government in the 1790s.

The Senate chamber on the second floor.
PHOTO COURTESY NATIONAL PARK SERVICE

In 1799 Washington's death was also commemorated in Congress Hall, when John Marshall referred to the late president as "first in war, first in peace and first in the hearts of his countrymen."

Congress Hall is also where the Bill of Rights was ratified. Park rangers give guided tours, starting out in the House chamber on the first floor before proceeding upstairs to the more ornate Senate chambers. Representatives sat on stiff wooden benches while senators were assigned individual comfy chairs. With two floors set aside for Congress, the Senate literally was the "upper" chamber while the House of Representatives was the "lower" chamber. As you ascend the stairs, stop on the landing and take a look out the arched window east for a unique view of Independence Hall as it's framed between the muntins.

With its dark green walls and barrel-vaulted ceiling, the Senate chamber is quite cozy. Although the country was growing, when the capital headed south to Washington there were still only 16 states so the room had to accommodate just 32 senators. Right outside the Senate room you'll see larger-than-life portraits of France's King Louis XVI and Marie Antoinette hanging on the wall in a committee room. It seems an odd juxtaposition for a seat of government that had just overthrown a hated monarchy. But as a park ranger pointed out, France, and its deposed royal family, were allies of the young nation.

Congress Hall Information

Address: 6th and Chestnut Streets

Hours: Daily, 9 a.m. to 5 p.m. Hours vary by season. Enter through the security booth at 5th and Chestnut Streets.

Admission: Free

Phone: (215) 965-2305

Website: nps.gov/inde/congress-hall.htm

Wheelchair accessibility: First floor only

Philosophical Hall
104 South 5th Street on Independence Square

The only privately owned building nestled on Independence Square, Philosophical Hall houses the museum of the American Philosophical Society, a scientific organization founded in 1743 by, you guessed it, Benjamin Franklin. The plain brick building was erected in 1789 based on a plan by Samuel Vaughan. It houses priceless artifacts related to America's founding including a draft of the **Declaration of Independence** written by Jefferson, along with his notes highlighting changes made by the Continental Congress.

The name of the organization conjures up images of learned men sitting around in togas à la ancient Greece discussing the latest musings by Socrates and Plato. But the reality is more down to earth. The group grew out of Franklin's **Leather Apron Club,** later known as the **Junto,** which he founded in 1727 as a small group for tradesmen to share their latest musings about how to better mankind, often over a tankard of ale.

Leather aprons worn by Junto members.

Out of these "spirit"-fueled meetings of the Junto sprouted ideas for the first volunteer fire company in Philadelphia, followed up by the first fire insurance company, the first hospital, improved street lighting, and more. While Franklin generally gets the credit for inventing these, he benefited greatly from chewing over the ideas first with his fellow Junto members. In a sign of his fairness, he didn't patent any of his inventions, such as the Franklin stove, so society could truly benefit from them.

In the 18th century men who sought scientific pursuits were called natural philosophers; the term "scientist" was not yet in vogue. The American Philosophical Society's mission was to "promote useful knowledge in America"—*useful* knowledge being key. The ever-practical Franklin abhorred the teaching of Latin and Greek. How was someone going to earn a living or contribute to society by devoting hours of precious time to learning how to speak a dead language?

I'm Your Venus

One of the greatest scientists that America produced was **David Rittenhouse,** who has a square named for him in a ritzy section of Philadelphia. History tends to place Rittenhouse in Franklin's shadow, but his achievements were stellar. When Franklin died, the leadership of the American Philosophical Society passed to Rittenhouse, who grew up on a farm outside Philadelphia and was self-taught in mathematics, astronomy, and scientific instrument making. He developed an intricate mechanical device called an orrery, which was as large as wide-screen, to accurately track the movements of the solar system. His true shining moment came in 1769 with the transit of Venus across the sun. This was a worldwide event that gave scientists the opportunity to calculate the distance from the Earth to the solar body. Rittenhouse organized a team to plot the movement of Venus, but at the key moment he promptly fainted from the excitement of it all. He recovered just in time to make a pretty accurate prediction of Earth's distance from the sun.

In 1797, the day before he became the vice president of the United States, Thomas Jefferson was named the president of the American Philosophical Society. The efficient multitasker didn't step down from this post until 1814, during which time he also managed to serve as the nation's president for eight years. This connection enhanced the society's collections. When President Jefferson initiated the **Lewis & Clark expedition** to explore the American West, he sent Meriwether Lewis to Philadelphia to learn about the latest advances in medicine from APS members Dr. Benjamin Rush and Dr. Caspar Wister. After the successful completion of the journey, Jefferson made sure that many of Lewis & Clarks' journals were given to the American Philosophical Society.

Philosophical Hall Information

Location: 104 S. 5th St.

Hours: Generally open from Apr through Dec for annual special exhibits, 10 a.m. to 4 p.m. Thurs through Sun. In 2015 and 2016 the special exhibits will focus on Thomas Jefferson. Check their website for details.

Admission: $2 donation appreciated

Phone: (215) 440-3440

Website: apsmuseum.org

Wheelchair accessibility: Use 5th Street entrance

Side Trip: Library Hall

Across the street from Philosophical Hall, at 105 S. 5th St., is the American Philosophical Society's current headquarters in Library Hall; it's a 1950s re-creation of the building that housed the Library Company of Philadelphia beginning in 1789. Founded by Benjamin Franklin in 1731, the Library Company was the first successful lending library in the country. The library's home was sketched out by William Thornton, a physician with no architectural background, who went on to design the US Capitol in Washington. It was demolished in 1889, but the reproduction façade is a fair example of Thornton's original graceful vision. Note the statue of **Benjamin Franklin,** looking resplendent in a toga, tucked into a niche over the doorway. The choice of clothing was selected by Franklin himself, a nod to the great classical thinkers of history. The figure was saved prior to the building's demolition; the original can be viewed at the Library Company's current headquarters at 1320 Locust St. Inside the foyer of Library Hall you'll find a rotating exhibit of finds from the American Philosophical Society's impressive collection of Americana that usually includes a journal from the Lewis & Clark expedition.

Side Trip: Declaration House (Graff's House)

Thomas Jefferson was a tenant at Jacob Graff's house when he was chosen to prepare the most famous document in American history. The 33-year-old delegate from Virginia chose the new home for his stay in Philadelphia during the Second Continental Congress because of its remote "country" location. It's hard to imagine now, but at the time the setting was a pastoral writer's retreat for Jefferson when he put quill to parchment in his second-floor apartment.

Thomas Jefferson.
PHOTO COURTESY INDEPENDENCE
NATIONAL HISTORICAL PARK

On June 11, 1776, the **Continental Congress** selected a **Committee of Five** to draft the document that would declare America's independence from Great Britain. The group consisted of: **Benjamin Franklin, John Adams, Thomas Jefferson, Robert Livingston Jr.,** and **Roger Sherman.**

Jefferson had already developed a reputation as a skilled writer so the members selected him to write the first draft of the document. The Committee of Five then edited the rough draft before presenting it to the Continental Congress for further revisions. Jefferson was a proud author and his private correspondence reveals that he was none too happy about many of the changes foisted on his handiwork. Either way, the final document was well received and its impact on American, and world, history unquestioned.

The original building was torn down in 1883 but photographs and other records existed to ensure accuracy when the National Park Service built the current replica in 1975. The two second-floor rooms where Jefferson spent many hours over the course of three weeks drafting the Declaration of Independence have been re-created to their appearance when he lived there. He was accompanied by a slave, 14-year-old Bob Hemings, who was the brother of Jefferson's reputed paramour, Sally Hemings. Jefferson devised a wooden lap desk for his writing, a copy of which is on display along with his swivel chair. Displays relay a timeline to writing the Declaration of Independence along with a brief movie.

The Declaration House is at 701 Market St. It's periodically closed due to federal government budget cuts so check ahead for visitor hours at (215) 965-2305 or nps.gov/inde/declaration-house.htm.

Pit Stop: Lore's Chocolates and Espresso Bar

Lore's is the sort of candy shop where your Aunt Bessie picked up chocolate bunnies and Halloween treats 50 years ago. Not much has changed—and that's good. When the Walter family purchased the business almost 30 years ago, they kept the Lore's tradition going.

Handmade chocolates molded in shapes to suit virtually any holiday, still made on site, are artfully displayed throughout the store. Buttercreams and caramels, lovingly rolled in either milk or dark chocolate, stand like sweet little toy soldiers on parade inside the original wood-and-glass cabinet, patiently waiting for one of the nice ladies working there to package them up in a pretty box. Consider trying some delectable chocolate-dipped pretzels—a sweet/salty/crunchy concoction that's the perfect pick-me-up during a trek along the Philadelphia Liberty Trail.

One recent addition is the take-out espresso bar next door, where you can get a frothy latte, mocha, or—naturally—hot chocolate.

Lore's Chocolates is located at 34 S. 7th St. and is open 9 a.m. to 5:30 p.m. Mon through Fri, 9 a.m. to 4 p.m. Sat. Closed Sun and the last two weeks of Aug.

Lore's Espresso Bar is located at 36 S. 7th St. and is open 6 a.m. to 4 p.m. Mon through Fri.

Side Trip: Philadelphia History Museum (formerly Atwater Kent Museum)

Philadelphia played such a pivotal role as the birthplace of America that sometimes its own city history gets lost in the process. This small museum chronicles the 300-plus year history of the City of Brotherly Love, putting the revolutionary events associated with it into context.

Through a series of permanent and rotating exhibits, select objects are presented in creative fashion. The museum reopened in 2012 after a three-year renovation, and now incorporates modern technology allowing for interactive displays, keeping all ages entertained.

The "Face to Facebook" gallery demonstrates the importance of personal likenesses and how they have evolved over the years, moving from hand-drawn images to daguerreotypes to photos. Visitors can even become part of the exhibit: Have a digital photo taken on site and your image will join portraits of **George Washington** painted by **Gilbert Stuart** in 1798 and African-American abolitionist **Harriet Lee Smith** from 1841.

George Washington stood here. The first president used the top of this desk to review papers and maps with his advisors.
PHOTO COURTESY PHILADELPHIA HISTORY MUSEUM

One of the highlights of the museum's collection is a wampum belt donated by the Penn family. Family lore has it that William Penn received the belt from the Lenni Lenape tribe in the 1680s, signifying peaceful relations between the Native Americans and Quakers. The desk used by President George Washington in the 1790s while living in the nearby President's House is also on display. Zooming forward a few hundred years, visitors can view boxing gloves worn by Philadelphia native **Joe Frazier** during a 1970 championship bout.

Kids will especially like the world's largest walkable map of Philadelphia, which dominates the floor of the main gallery. This is one place where parents can encourage kids to "play in the streets." Exhibits on the surrounding walls showcase historic events, including their location on the map at your feet.

The museum also offers a series of educational programs for visiting school groups, including the critically acclaimed anti-slavery presentation **"Quest for Freedom,"** which is part of the National Underground Railroad Network to Freedom from the National Park Service. Contact the museum for more information.

The Philadelphia History Museum is located at 15 S. 7th St. Hours are generally 10:30 a.m. to 4:30 p.m. Tues through Sat. Updated information is available at (215) 685-4830 or philadelphiahistory.org/index.php.

WASHINGTON SQUARE AND SOCIETY HILL

Let's explore the neighborhood where so many of the Revolution's pivotal figures spent their daily lives. Take a constitutional through the leafy streets of Society Hill to get a sense of 18th-century Philadelphia as a place where people lived, shopped, worshipped, cured their ailments, and entertained.

The posh neighborhood takes its name from the **Free Society of Traders,** a real-estate development and trading company to which William Penn granted the initial parcels of land in this area. (The word "Society" as used here had nothing to do with its upscale connotation; it was just another way of saying corporation or company. But somehow

Bricks and shutters are right at home in Society Hill.

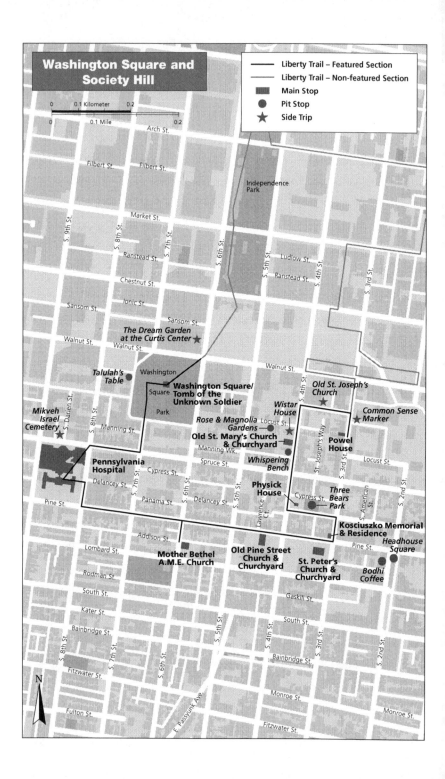

Washington Square and Society Hill

Liberty Trail – Featured Section
Liberty Trail – Non-featured Section
Main Stop
Pit Stop
Side Trip

0   0.1 Kilometer   0.2
0   0.1 Mile   0.2

Arch St.

Filbert St.   Filbert St.

Market St.

S. 9th St.
S. 8th St.
S. 7th St.
S. 6th St.
S. 5th St.
S. 4th St.
S. 3rd St.

Ranstead St.

Independence Park

Ludlow St.

Ranstead St.

Chestnut St.

Sansom St.   Ionic St.

Sansom St.

The Dream Garden at the Curtis Center ★

Walnut St.   Walnut St.

Walnut St.

Talulah's Table ●

Washington

Washington Square/ Tomb of the Unknown Soldier

Old St. Joseph's Church ★

S. Darien St.
S. 8th St.

Mikveh Israel Cemetery ★

Square Park

Wistar House

Common Sense Marker ★

Manning St.

Rose & Magnolia Gardens ●
Locust St.

Old St. Mary's Church & Churchyard ●

Locust St.

Powel House

Pennsylvania Hospital

Manning Wk.

Spruce St.

Whispering Bench

St. Joseph's Way
S. 3rd St.

Locust St.

Cypress St.

Physick House

Three Bears Park

S. 2nd St.

Delancey St.
S. 7th St.

Panama St.

Delancey St.
S. 6th St.
S. 5th St.

Cypress St.

Lawrence Ct.

S. American St.

Pine St.

Kosciuszko Memorial & Residence

Addison St.

Pine St.

Headhouse Square ●

Lombard St.

Mother Bethel A.M.E. Church

Old Pine Street Church & Churchyard

St. Peter's Church & Churchyard

Bodhi Coffee ●

Rodman St.

South St.

Kater St.

Gaskill St.

Bainbridge St.
S. 8th St.
S. 7th St.
S. 6th St.

South St.
S. 5th St.
S. 4th St.
S. 3rd St.

Fitzwater St.

Bainbridge St.
S. 2nd St.

N

Fulton St.

E. Passyunk Ave.

Monroe St.

Fitzwater St.

Monroe St.

"Corporation Hill" doesn't have the same ring.) Due to business setbacks, by the 1720s the Free Society had withered away, but their name lives on in this community filled with 18th-century homes.

If Benjamin Franklin returned to Philadelphia today, some parts of Society Hill would look familiar to him, but that couldn't be said if he had returned in the mid-20th century. Although the neighborhood boasted some of the most elegant mansions of the federal era, by the 1950s it was run down and ripe for urban renewal. Rather than raze the neighborhood, a popular urban renewal tactic at the time, historic preservationists, city planners, and political forces joined together to rebuild the community. Society Hill looks like it could be part of a movie set, and some streets did have cameo roles in the film *National Treasure*.

The northwestern anchor of the neighborhood is **Washington Square,** one of the five squares laid out in William Penn's original vision for Philadelphia. Although it served time as a cemetery, it's now a wooded urban oasis. We're certain Penn would approve.

Start this portion of the Philadelphia Liberty Trail at the square, looping your way gradually south and east. This tour encompasses open space, green walkways, the first hospital in America, historic churches (including one that was a precursor to the Civil Rights movement) and fabulous mansions. Along the way we'll amble through the largest grouping of 18th-century architecture in America and finish inside the home where **George and Martha Washington** celebrated their 20th wedding anniversary at a grand soiree in the ballroom.

One Degree of Kevin Bacon

The catalyst for the renovation of Society Hill was nationally known city planner **Edmund Bacon.** Not only did he make the cover of *Time* magazine for his efforts, he's also the father of actor, and Philadelphia native, **Kevin Bacon.**

Washington Square

6th and Walnut Streets

> No Walden sky was ever more blue than the roof of
> Washington Square this morning.
>
> —*Christopher Morley,* Travels in Philadelphia, *1920*

When **William Penn** laid out his "greene Country Towne" in 1683
this square bore the more prosaic moniker Southeast Square. Naming it after George Washington didn't come until 1825. Despite initial
plans for an idyllic square, in 1705 the city's common council identified
the need for a "stranger burying ground" for visitors dying in the city.
(Quite a way to boost tourism!)

Washington Square was an active burial site for almost a century,
especially during the sporadic smallpox and yellow fever outbreaks in

Washington Square's calm setting.

Philadelphia. During the yellow fever epidemic of 1793, which killed an estimated 10 percent of the city's population, bodies were quickly bagged in canvas before being lowered into the ground.

The square was also a gathering spot for both free blacks and slaves, earning it the nickname Congo Square. Historian John Fanning Watson wrote in 1833, "Many can still remember when the slaves were allowed the last days of the fairs for their jubilee . . . after the customs of their several nations in Africa."

During the Revolution it was the final resting place for soldiers from both sides of the conflict. According to a note that John Adams penned in April 1777, the vast majority of those deaths were not battle related: "I took a walk into the 'Potter's Field,' a burying ground between the new stone prison and the hospital. . . . Disease had destroyed ten men for us where the sword of the enemy has killed one!" When the British occupied Philadelphia in September 1777, they converted the Walnut Street Jail across the street into a prisoner-of-war facility; captive American soldiers who died from the squalid conditions there were buried in the square alongside deceased British troops.

That's One Small Sapling for Man, One Giant Leaf for Mankind

In Washington Square make it your mission to find the **"moon tree."** In the years leading up to the Bicentennial in 1976, trees that were germinated from seeds that astronaut **Stuart Roosa** brought along on **Apollo 14** were planted across America. The sycamore moon tree on Washington Square died in 2008 and for several years a bronze plaque commemorated a dead tree. A new one was planted in 2011 from a clone of the original. The plaque stating that the tree was planted on May 6, 1975, remains, but it obviously doesn't refer to the sapling it now marks.

Memorial to Washington and the Unknown Soldier of the American Revolution.

Thanks to the efforts of a noted French botanist named François André Michaux, the bucolic setting you see today doesn't bear any of the marks of its prior morbid uses. In 1815 he began planting over 50 different species of trees to create the wooded setting that Penn had originally envisioned.

On the western edge of the 6-acre park stands the **Washington Memorial,** a full-size bronze sculpture of its namesake gazing off toward Independence Hall. Etched into the stone wall behind Washington is the statement, "In unmarked graves within this square lie thousands of unknown soldiers of Washington's army who died of wounds and sickness during the Revolutionary War."

At the feet of Washington lie a stone sarcophagus and eternal flame honoring the **Unknown Soldier of the American Revolution.** Flags of the original 13 colonies flutter in the breeze along the walkway approaching the memorial. It's both somber and uplifting to

William Penn's Greene Country Towne

Although the grid pattern of Philadelphia looks fairly normal today, it was pretty revolutionary when William Penn first laid it out in 1683. The core of the city was a 1,200-acre site bordered by the Delaware and Schuylkill Rivers to the east and west, and Vine and South Streets to the north and south. The north-south axis of Broad Street and the east-west line of High (now Market) Street bisected the plan. These two main thoroughfares were 100 feet across, making them wider than any street in London.

Despite living his early years on gentlemen's estates and the serpentine alleys of old London, Penn proved he was a visionary by developing a city plan that allowed for orderly, controlled growth. Visitors to 18th-century Philadelphia uniformly commented on the "streets that met at right angles." Penn's surveyor, fellow Quaker Thomas Holme, also allocated space for four square-shaped urban parks. Although they were unnamed in the original plan they are now known as Washington, Franklin, Rittenhouse, and Logan Squares. A fifth square was set aside for municipal uses in the center of the plan; it's where City Hall now stands at the intersection of Broad and Market Streets.

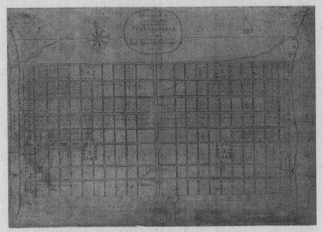

Penn's revolutionary plan for a future revolutionary city.
PHOTO COURTESY THE LIBRARY COMPANY OF PHILADELPHIA

take a moment to honor these fallen, America's first freedom fighters. The Sons of the American Revolution participates in commemorative services with full color guard at the tomb each year on Washington's Birthday and Memorial Day.

Today Washington Square is a sylvan respite from the tourist flocks gathering across the street at Independence Hall. On sunny days take advantage of the tree-shaded benches and grounds to rest weary feet that have been trampling over cobblestone paths, an appropriate use that pays homage to William Penn's original plan for this green piece of Philadelphia.

Washington Square Information

Location: 6th and Walnut Streets

Hours: Always open

Admission: Free

Wheelchair accessibility: The square is accessible, complete with smooth, paved walkways.

Pit Stop: A Picnic in Washington Square

Step into **Talula's Daily,** an upscale neighborhood cafe and market that offers coffees, pastries, and premade lunches perfect for enjoying a picnic in Washington Square. The cafe is hard to spot since signage is subdued on this predominantly noncommercial square. You'll find it in the Art Deco building on the street behind the statue of George Washington. Talula's entrance is to the right of the lobby. If the weather isn't cooperating, you can enjoy your lunch or snack at one of Talula's communal tables inside.

Talula's Daily is located at 208 Washington Sq. West and is open seven days a week from 7 a.m. to 7 p.m.; talulasdaily.com. (*Note:* Don't confuse this cafe with Talula's Garden, its more formal sister restaurant down the block. For more information about Talula's Garden, see the **Where to Eat** section.)

Pennsylvania Hospital
South 8th Street, between Spruce and Pine

Hospitals are not typically listed in guidebooks as sights to visit, but this one is definitely worth a look. Pennsylvania Hospital is America's oldest, dating back to 1751. Although it is still a working hospital the squeamish need not worry. There are no creepy jars of preserved organs or primitive surgical instruments lurking about. Instead, the building and grounds sport some excellent examples of colonial-era art, architecture, and gardens.

By the mid 1700s, Philadelphia was the fastest-growing city in the 13 colonies. However, prosperity brought massive immigration,

The dome on the building on the left allowed light into the nation's first surgical amphitheater.

crowding, and new diseases to town and there were inadequate facilities to treat the sick. **Dr. Thomas Bond** conceived the hospital in 1750 and brought the proposal to his friend Benjamin Franklin for assistance in acquiring capital for the project.

Many American firsts are credited to Pennsylvania Hospital, including the first medical library, apothecary, and surgical amphitheater. The foremost physicians of the day practiced here. **Dr. Benjamin Rush,** the father of American psychiatry (and a signer of the Declaration of Independence), spent 30 years on the medical staff.

The Pine Building was built in three sections between 1752 and 1804. Designed by Samuel Rhoads, it's considered one of the finest examples of colonial and federal architecture in the city. Its Great Court displays portraits of early medical luminaries, along with an 18th-century fire engine. A rare **David Rittenhouse** tall-case planetary clock dating from 1787, in its day perhaps the most technologically advanced clock in America, is tucked into a meeting room that was once the original apothecary.

The library commands center stage on the second floor of the court. The first medical library in the United States, it was designated the country's most important medical library by the American Medical Association in 1847. The early 19th-century room echoes with 200 years of medical research. Over 13,000 historical volumes on medicine, science, and natural history line the shelves of glass-fronted cabinets on the main floor and gallery. See if you can spot any **incunabula** (we don't often get to use that word, so we just had to highlight it); these are books printed before 1501.

Climb to the third floor to view the nation's first surgical amphitheater. The circular room does indeed resemble a theater; benched boxes line the wall in multiple tiers. But the large table in the center, drawing light from windows above, reveals the room's true purpose. Starting in 1807, airy skylights in the dome allowed surgery to be performed using daylight to illuminate the proceedings. However, anesthesia was not used until the 1840s. According to historians at Pennsylvania Hospital, prior to that surgeons got patients "blind drunk, gave them opium or administered a sharp tap on the head with a mallet, enough to render the patient unconscious and hopefully not dead." Advanced for the time, but still enough to make 21st-century visitors cringe.

Science meets art in Benjamin West's massive painting, ***Christ Healing the Sick in the Temple,*** occupying pride-of-place in a special pavilion connecting the Pine Building with the modern-day hospital. West donated the masterpiece to the hospital in 1817 in lieu of a contribution of cash. As one of the preeminent artists of the day, West's picture caused a sensation. The hospital charged a small fee to view it and over the next 25 years raised $15,000, well in excess of any cash West might have donated.

The Pine Building is fronted by a landscaped circular drive that flowers with tulips, wisteria, azaleas, and other perennials throughout the warmer months. Movie fans will recognize this as the setting where

Rocky and Adrian first introduced their baby boy to the world in *Rocky II*. Gazing serenely over it all is a statue of William Penn, placed here in 1804—after being discovered by one of his descendants in a London antique shop.

Before you leave seek out the cornerstone of the original building, somewhat hidden at the base of the east wing. Laid in 1755, its flowery inscription was drafted by Benjamin Franklin. Although "George the Second Happily Reigning" may no longer apply, over 250 years later some of Ben's words, including "for the relief of the sick and miserable," still ring true.

Pennsylvania Hospital Information

Location: 8th Street, just south of Spruce Street

Hours: 9 a.m. to 4 p.m. Mon through Fri (last admission is 3:30 p.m.)

Admission: Free, but a self-guided tour brochure is available for purchase in the hospital gift shop adjacent to the lobby for a suggested donation of $4. Enter via the hospital's main entrance on 8th Street. Guided tours between 9 a.m. and 4 p.m. can be arranged through the hospital's library with 48 hours' notice for a suggested donation of $4 per person. Tours last approximately 1 hour. Call the library during normal business hours for further information.

Phone: (215) 829-3370

Website: uphs.upenn.edu/paharc

Wheelchair accessibility: Both *Christ Healing the Sick at the Temple* and the gardens are wheelchair accessible. The remaining attractions are not.

Side Trip: Mikveh Israel Cemetery

Attracted by William Penn's "great experiment" welcoming people of all religions, Jewish immigrants were drawn to Philadelphia. The Mikveh Israel congregation is the oldest Jewish community in Philadelphia and the second oldest in the nation. It began with this small cemetery, tucked away behind a high brick wall, where many prominent and patriotic Jews from the 18th century are buried.

In 1740, **Nathan Levy** applied to Thomas Penn for a plot of land to bury his infant son with a proper Jewish ceremony. He was granted this lot on the north side of Spruce Street near 9th Street, which became a Jewish communal cemetery. The year of the grant is considered the founding date of the Mikveh Israel congregation, whose name means "Hope of Israel."

Active in political affairs, three members of the congregation, merchants Mathias Bush, Moses Mordecai, and Barnard Gratz, signed

The oldest Jewish cemetery in Pennsylvania.

the 1765 Non-Importation Resolutions that opposed the Stamp Act imposed by Great Britain. By 1775, there were 300 Jewish people among the city's population of 35,000. Mikveh Israel's location in Philadelphia earned it the sobriquet "The Synagogue of the American Revolution." Indeed, Benjamin Franklin and Robert Morris are listed as friends of the congregation.

There are several prominent people buried in the cemetery: Nathan Levy, who along with David Franks formed the first Jewish business partnership in America; **Rebecca Gratz,** who is considered, somewhat tenuously, to have been the inspiration for the Jewish heroine Rebecca in Sir Walter Scott's novel *Ivanhoe;* and **Phillip Moses Russell,** who performed heroically when he was on George Washington's medical staff during the winter at Valley Forge.

Although his actual burial spot within the cemetery is unknown, revolutionary patriot **Haym Solomon** is honored with a granite marker at the main gate; born in Poland, the finance broker immigrated to New York in 1772. The British arrested him for spying in 1776 but he was spared the noose when they used him as a translator for Hessian troops. After encouraging many of them to desert the army, he was arrested yet again and sentenced to death.

Solomon escaped to Philadelphia where he helped the Continental Congress fill its coffers for the war effort, advancing his own money to the cause and loaning money to several members of the Continental Congress including James Madison. Despite his business success, Salomon died in 1785 a pauper, his family claiming that the government hadn't repaid him.

In 1975 the United States government recognized Solomon's efforts to help finance the American Revolution. His likeness was featured on a 10-cent postage stamp for the Bicentennial in a series called "Contributors to the Cause." While that doesn't sound like much now, at the time it was the cost to mail a first-class letter.

Hours: The wrought-iron gates set into the circa-1803 brick wall are usually locked. To set up a tour call the synagogue office at (215) 922-5446. The current Mikveh Israel congregation is in a contemporary building at 44 N. 4th St., near the National Museum of American Jewish History.

Mother Bethel A.M.E. Church and Richard Allen Museum
419 South 6th Street

Hearing the name "Mother Bethel" attached to a church calls to mind a kindly old woman gently patting children on the head, like Mother Teresa. But this church is not named for an individual; rather it is the founding site, the "mother church," of the **African Methodist Episcopal (A.M.E.) Church.** The events leading up to the creation of

The current Mother Bethel was built in 1890. The site is the longest continually owned by African Americans in the country.

Mother Bethel are considered to be the first assertion of civil rights by African Americans.

During the 18th century the Methodist teachings of John Wesley spread throughout the colonies. Wesley abhorred slavery, and an overall belief in racial equality made the Methodist church popular among both freed and enslaved blacks.

By the 1780s African-American preachers, most notably **Richard Allen** and **Absalom Jones,** were active in integrated parishes in Philadelphia. Allen's preaching of the 5 a.m. Sunday service at nearby St. George's United Methodist Church grew in popularity, bringing in many new African-American members.

Ironically, the church's popularity as a site of racial equality caused a rift in the congregation. When church elders mandated segregated seating due to the growing numbers of black parishioners, Allen and Jones led a walkout of most of the African-American contingent in 1792. These black "protestants" were among the very first civil rights activists in America.

The Blacksmith Shop Meeting House was established in 1794 on the site of the present Mother Bethel building, with Richard Allen as pastor. It was soon renamed Bethel Church, meaning "gathering of souls." In 1816 a meeting of African Methodist church leaders met here and the African Methodist Episcopal denomination was born. Henceforth, this church of humble origins that began in a former blacksmith shop would be known as Mother Bethel, designating it as the founding church of the A.M.E. order.

Throughout its 200-plus-year history, Mother Bethel has been a center for African-American community and culture in the New World, and a vital part of the American landscape. The church was active in recruiting patriots for the War of 1812 and for the Union Army during the Civil War. Mother Bethel, along with other A.M.E. churches in the city, played a pivotal role on the Underground Railroad; **Harriet Tubman attended services here.**

Today visitors can tour the sanctuary, as well as a museum on the lower level of the church. The museum contains the tomb of Reverend Richard Allen, himself a freed slave, along with artifacts and displays about his life and accomplishments. Exhibits about the role of Mother Bethel and African Americans throughout history, including the Underground Railroad, occur on a rotating basis.

Stop in to tour the sanctuary and museum, or better yet, attend an uplifting service on a Sunday morning. Although there is no actual "Mother Bethel," you might just get a kindly old lady to pat you on the head.

Mother Bethel A.M.E. Church Information

Location: 419 S. 6th St.

Hours: The museum is open 10 a.m. to 3 p.m. and after services on Sunday. Walk-ins are welcome, but groups should request a tour via the website.

Admission: Free, but donations are encouraged.

Phone: (215) 925-0616

Website: motherbethel.org

Wheelchair accessibility: Not wheelchair accessible.

Old Pine Street Church and Graveyard
412 Pine Street

Old Pine, or, as it's officially known, Third Scots and Mariners Presbyterian, is the only Presbyterian church from the colonial era still standing in Philadelphia. Hidden away inside the current Greek Revival structure is the original circa-1768 brick building. Noted architect Robert Smith was awarded the commission to design the church.

The precariously leaning fence from 1835 was designed by John Haviland.

During the British occupation of Philadelphia, the invading army converted Old Pine into a hospital. The pews, flooring, pulpit, and decorative woodwork were burned to produce heat. The British soldiers were a bit more aggressive in their destruction of Old Pine than they were to neighboring churches, a likely response to pastor George Duffield's dual role as the chaplain to the First Continental Congress in 1774 and providing comfort to the American troops at Valley Forge during the British occupation of Philadelphia.

It didn't help matters that John Adams also attended Old Pine, which earned it the nickname "the church of the patriots." This was a time when

---

Not Exactly Six Feet Under
In order to conserve space, bodies are buried in stacks at depths of 3, 6, and 9 feet.

Thirteen-star flags honor the Revolutionary War soldiers buried here.

members of Parliament in London referred to the American insurrection as the "Presbyterian War." It was easier for them to comprehend the uprising through the prism of England's longtime conflicts with Presbyterian Scotland and not their fellow Anglicans; that just wouldn't be "veddy" British. The interior was left a shambles and rebuilt after the war.

Several notables are buried here, including Jared Ingersoll, a signer of the US Constitution, along with 235 men who fought in the American Revolution (their graves are marked with a striking tableau of 13-star American flags flapping in the breeze).

Old Pine Street Church Information

Location: 412 Pine St.

Hours: Service on Sun 10:30 a.m.; office hours 8:30 a.m. to 4:30 p.m. Mon through Fri. The churchyard is open dawn to dusk daily. Tours of the church and graveyard are available if arranged a week in advance. A suitable donation is appreciated. You can view a video of a graveyard tour at oldpineconservancy .org.

Admission: Free

Phone: (215) 925-8051

Website: oldpine.org

Wheelchair accessibility: Both the church and churchyard are wheelchair accessible. To enter the church, phone ahead so a ramp can be placed at the side door.

Scavenger Hunt

Hey kids, if you happen to visit Philadelphia on a rainy day you're in luck. Splash away in puddles and look for the decorative wrought-iron boot scrapes huddled by the steps to many of the houses. These were used when unpaved streets left mud all over colonial boots and shoes. And since people weren't getting around by car back then, horses were also contributing something else to the mud.

Into the mud.

Thaddeus Kosciuszko National Memorial
301 Pine Street

A war cannot be won without strong military fortifications, and for these the Continental Army owed thanks to **Thaddeus Kosciuszko.** The Polish military engineer lived for a time at this small Georgian-era rooming house in Society Hill.

Kosciuszko (pronounced "kah-shoo-sko") studied military science and engineering in both his native Poland and Paris before the American fight for freedom lured him to the colonies in 1776. Shortly after arriving in Philadelphia, Kosciuszko volunteered his services to the fledgling American government; his unique expertise prompted the Continental Congress to offer him a commission as colonel of engineers.

Throughout the Revolution Kosciuszko oversaw the design and building of defenses that protected ports and helped stave off the British

The boardinghouse where Kosciuszko stayed in 1797.

Army. Kosciuszko's fortifications along the Hudson River are credited with aiding the victory at the Battle of Saratoga and the successful blockade at West Point. For his contributions to the war effort George Washington promoted Kosciuszko to Brigadier General of the Army in 1783. Kosciuszko also received American citizenship.

Armed with revolutionary fervor, Kosciuszko returned to his native Poland in 1784 with hopes of helping his own country gain independence. After initial successes, the Russians defeated the Poles in 1794 and Kosciuszko was imprisoned.

Upon his release, Kosciuszko returned to America in 1797 to a hero's welcome, living in this small rooming house at 3rd and Pine Streets. He socialized with friends from his Revolutionary War days, many of whom were now bigwigs in the new government. He spent significant time with his friend Thomas Jefferson, who helped him draft his will and agreed to become its executor.

Kosciuszko was an ardent abolitionist. Upon his death in 1817, Kosciuszko bequeathed over $10,000 (more than $175,000 today) to Jefferson for the express purpose of freeing slaves and establishing them in skilled employment. In an unusual twist, Jefferson declined the bequest and avoided honoring his friend's wish.

The Thaddeus Kosciuszko National Memorial is not a large museum; in fact, at 0.02 acres, the National Park Service lists it as the smallest of its sites. Inside the former boardinghouse are displays of Kosciuszko's military fortifications; the furnished room where he met with Jefferson, Dr. Benjamin Rush, and others; as well as information

---

Thaddeus Kosciuszko National Memorial Information

Location: 301 Pine St.

Hours: Noon to 4 p.m. Sat and Sun.

Admission: Free

Phone: (215) 965-2305

Website: nps.gov/thko

Wheelchair accessibility: The first floor of the building is accessible. Please call in advance to ensure admission via the wheelchair entrance. Restrooms on the second floor are not wheelchair accessible.

Note: If after visiting the Kosciuszko Memorial you are hankering for more Polish activities, the Polish American Cultural Center is just 2 blocks north at 308 Walnut St. For more information go to: polishamericancenter.org

---

about his military exploits in Poland. A short film gives an overview of his life; it may be the only one in the National Park System that offers narrative in both English and Polish.

St. Peter's Church and Churchyard
313 Pine Street

By the mid-18th century, Philadelphia was expanding so rapidly that churches could barely keep up with the population growth. More homes were being built in Society Hill, and Christ Church on High (now Market) Street was becoming too crowded. Parishioners rented boxes in the church for seating, which were now full at Christ Church. With no room for new worshippers, another church, St. Peter's, was planned in Society Hill. **Bishop William White,** whose home is on the Philadelphia Liberty Trail, became the rector; he held the position at both St. Peter's and Christ Churches until he died in 1836.

To See or Not to See

St. Peter's was built during the Age of Enlightenment, which favored clear glass windows in churches, a design that was supposed to encourage free thought. Some religious leaders believed that stained-glass windows depicting biblical scenes were déclassé, an outmoded method for indoctrinating the masses. There was certainly a lot of "outside the box" thinking going on in 18th-century Philadelphia.

Ironically the pendulum of ideas on this subject swung in the opposite direction a century later when, in a burst of neo-Gothic fervor, St. Peter's installed colorful stained glass of the type they had originally opposed. But there is nothing as constant as change: In preparation for the American Bicentennial in 1976 the stained glass was removed from the side windows and replaced with clear glass once more.

The setting of St. Peter's is so idyllic it's hard to believe you're in a major American city.

Thomas and Richard Penn, sons of William Penn, donated the land for the new church. Architect Robert Smith paid homage to these patrons with the Penn family crest, visible just above the church's wineglass-shaped pulpit. The interior is a monochromatic blanket of white punctuated with gold accents, all highlighted by stark sunlight streaming in through the clear glass windows.

The box pews were designed with high walls to keep parishioners warm in the days before central heating. One of the more prominent pews belonged to **Mayor Samuel Powel** and his wife **Elizabeth,** who sometimes brought along **George and Martha Washington** as their guests. St. Peter's is unusual because its pulpit is on the west end of the building, while the altar is to the east. The congregation begins services facing the pulpit for "The Liturgy of the Word"—Bible readings, sermon, and prayers—before shifting in their seats to turn eastward toward the altar for communion.

St. Peter's celebrated its 250th anniversary in 2011 with a series of commemorative events, including resurrecting an original prayer book out of the archives; it revealed the places where in 1776 King George's name had been crossed out whenever he was mentioned in a prayer.

Due to the church's long history there are many prominent people buried in the churchyard. They include:

- **Nicholas Biddle,** head of the controversial Second Bank of the United States.
- Philadelphia native **George Mifflin Dallas,** the 11th vice president of the United States under James Polk. His memory lives on in history by being the namesake for Dallas, Texas.
- **Commodore Stephen Decatur,** naval hero against the Barbary pirates at the Battle of Tripoli and later in the War of 1812; he died in a duel at age 41 with a fellow US Navy commodore, James Barron.
- **Samuel Fraunces,** George Washington's steward and the proprietor of the famed **Fraunces Tavern** in New York and Philadelphia.
- The **eight Indian tribal chieftains** who were invited to Philadelphia by President George Washington to discuss boundary

disputes in the Northwest Territory, but died of smallpox during their sojourn in 1793.

- **Colonel John Nixon,** whose name crops up in so many stories in colonial Philadelphia. He gave the first public reading of the Declaration of Independence on July 8, 1776.
- **Charles Willson Peale,** who painted the first portrait of George Washington, along with many other paintings that now hang on the walls nearby in the Portrait Gallery of the Second Bank of the United States.

St. Peter's Church and Churchyard Information

Location: 313 Pine St.

Hours: The church building is open 8 a.m. to 4 p.m. Mon to Fri, 8 a.m. to 3 p.m. Sat and Sun. Guides are generally available 11 a.m. to 3 p.m. Sat and 1 to 3 p.m. on Sun. The churchyard is open early morning to dusk daily. Services are 9 a.m. and 11 a.m. on Sun.

Admission: Free

Phone: (215) 925-5968

Website: stpetersphila.org

Wheelchair accessibility: The church and paths in the churchyard are accessible.

Note: A free audio tour of the church and churchyard is available by calling (215) 554-6161 on your cell phone or by downloading an MP3 of the tour at: stpetersphila.org/history.html.

Pit Stop: Headhouse Square and Bodhi Coffee

In the mood for some shopping, 18th-century style? Wander over to Headhouse Square at 2nd and Pine Streets, which has been a market destination since 1745. It was originally known as "Newmarket" to distinguish it from its older counterpart on High (now Market) Street.

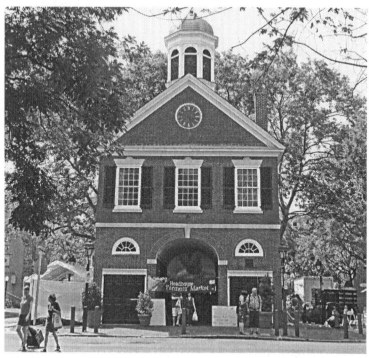

Shoppers have been purchasing local farm products at Headhouse Square for over 250 years.

The eponymous "Headhouse" was constructed in 1805 as a firehouse addition to the original market building and is a superb example of federal architecture. The long, narrow brick pavilion behind the Headhouse is known as the "Shambles," an old English word for a meat market. The Shambles was reconstructed in the 1960s, but still retains colonial styling.

Stop by on Sunday mornings between May and December for the weekly farmers' market. It's the largest weekly outdoor market in the city, boasting fresh fruits, vegetables, cheeses, artisanal chocolates, and other delectable treats from nearby farms. *USA Today* selected it as one of the "10 best spots for foodies." Take along a sack and imagine you're buying apples alongside old Ben himself.

The surrounding square is filled with an assortment of restaurants and pubs in period buildings. For a quick snack try **Bodhi Coffee.** The low-key baristas brew your beverage with scientific precision. Take a seat in the window overlooking the Shambles and refresh yourself with a pastry or sandwich before resuming your walk back in time.

Headhouse Square is located along 2nd Street, between Pine and Lombard Streets. The Headhouse Farmers' Market is open Sun from 9 a.m. to 2 p.m. between May and Dec. Check thefoodtrust.org for a list of exact dates and vendors.

Bodhi Coffee is at 410 S. 2nd St. and is open Mon to Fri 7 a.m. to 7 p.m., Sat 8 a.m. to 7 p.m., and Sun 8 a.m. to 5 p.m.

📷 *pit stop: Three Bears park (Delancey park)*

If all this historic immersion has young visitors a bit fidgety, pop into Three Bears Park and work off some youthful energy. The pocket park is a cozy little gem tucked away behind the Physick House. Delancey is one of Philadelphia's prettiest streets, lined with beautifully restored colonial-era houses and shady trees. This cobblestoned, 3-block-long

Kids love coloring the polar bears with chalk.

section of Delancey Street gets very little traffic, making this park a family-friendly destination.

Officially named Delancey Park, Three Bears Park offers a modern play gym and a set of swings, all on a soft, bouncy surface. Kids can climb on the polar bears from which the park gets its name. Plenty of benches for un-fidgety parents line the playground, and there are a few picnic tables if you've brought lunch or a snack.

Three Bears Park is located on Delancey Street, between 3rd and 4th Streets, and is open seven days a week. For more information check threebearspark.org.

Physick House
321 South 4th Street

The circa-1786 Physick House is the only freestanding federal home that remains in Society Hill. The imposing 29-room structure's origins were a bit more modest than it appears today. In the 1770s it was a simple brick affair, occupied by **Colonel John Nixon,** the orator who first read the Declaration of Independence to the public. (Interesting side note for presidential history buffs: Nixon's father was named Richard, and both he and the 37th president were Quakers.)

Wine importer Henry Hill purchased the property in 1782 and added onto it, creating one of the finest homes in Philadelphia. Hill

---

Just Hanging Around

Colonel John Nixon was living in the forerunner to the Physick House when he read the Declaration of Independence in public for the first time on July 8, 1776. Dr. Physick recalls the incident from when he was eight years old. He was playing in the woods behind the State House and heard someone yell at the end of the reading, "You're all going to hang for this!" There's one in every crowd.

The delightful fan window over the door was imported from England.

had discovered a crafty loophole to avoid the British tariffs on alcohol shipped from Europe. Madeira wine, produced on a Portuguese island off the coast of Africa, was exempt from taxation, providing an 18th-century version of duty-free booze that was popular in local taverns.

Hill loosened the purse strings when he expanded the house; the original part where Nixon lived became the kitchen, a role it still serves. In the front of the house Hill made a statement about his success to townsfolk passing by: Notice the double-width front entry door with the huge fanlight above it. The ornate window (with still-intact original glass) was imported in one piece from England, and was reportedly the largest in Pennsylvania.

The aptly named **Dr. Philip Syng Physick** purchased the house in 1815. (His maternal grandfather, Philip Syng, was the silversmith who crafted the inkwell that was used to sign the Declaration of Independence.) After studying medicine in Edinburgh, Physick returned to Philadelphia where he set up a medical practice with **Dr. Benjamin Rush,** one of the Declaration's signers who used Grandpa Syng's inkwell for the event.

Physick was appointed the first professor of surgery at the University of Pennsylvania medical school and is credited with several

The Pompeii-themed wallpaper in the foyer comes from the same French factory that's been producing it for two centuries.

inventions, including an improved splint to treat thigh fractures and an instrument for the removal of tonsils. Many of his medical and dental devices are on display in the home and closely resemble modern surgical equipment.

The home, which remained in the family until 1941, retains a host of original furnishings and is decorated in the federal and French-influenced Empire styles; it reflects Physick's upper-crust tastes and wealth.

One of the highlights is an unusual oval mahogany document press in the breakfast room. Despite its Art Deco appearance, the piece originally belonged to William Penn's son John. Dr. Physick's father Edmund acquired it from John Penn after he returned to England. With its impeccable provenance, can you imagine bringing it to the *Antiques Roadshow*?

The second-floor ceilings are an impressive 13 feet tall. Most of the furnishings in these rooms are original, right down to the original silk fabric on the sofa on which Physick reclined. An embroidered sampler on the wall was stitched in 1740 by Abigail Syng, Physick's mother, when she was 10 years old and has remained in the family ever since. Physick himself lived in the house until he died in 1837.

The "Pop" of American Soda

Dr. Philip Syng Physick was more than just the "Father of American Surgery." In 1807 the good doctor created an artificially carbonated water to cure his patients of stomach upsets. He was purveying "plop, plop, fizz, fizz, oh what a relief it is" years before Alka-Seltzer entered the market. The cost of the daily soda regimen was $1.50 per month. To enhance the taste Physick directed the pharmacist to add sweet fruit syrup to the beverage, creating America's first soda. In 2007 his descendant Del Conner reintroduced the beverage, which visitors can purchase during their tour of the house.

Tours are offered today by Del Conner, a descendant of Dr. Physick. With his family's heritage, he imparts a unique insight and familiarity with the home. Many of the heirlooms you'll see are ones he grew up with. As a child he even played with one of the naval swords on display; it was presented at Independence Hall to his great-great-grandfather Commodore David Conner for gallantry during the War of 1812.

Side Trip: Have a Secret Conversation

A block north of the Physick House, at the intersection of Manning and South 4th Streets, you'll find a curved bench built into a brick wall along the sidewalk. This is a reproduction of a traditional **Whispering Bench,** which proved a clever way to hold a private conversation in public.

In colonial times, when a young man and woman were courting (or dating, or going out, or in a relationship, or hooking up, depending on which decade you're from) they weren't allowed to put their heads together for a private chat. They sought spots like this bench where they could "date" out in plain sight without having to endure the "tsk tsk" of strict colonial matrons. The unique curved design of the bench allowed quiet voices to travel from one side to the other without anyone else hearing the conversation.

This phenomenon exists in many structures with a curved shape, including the domed rotunda of the US Capitol and the curved gallery of St. Paul's Cathedral in London.

Young visitors will enjoy trading "secret messages." Simply sit on opposite ends of the bench and speak into the curved wall with a normal voice.

Old St. Mary's Church and Churchyard
252 South 4th Street

In 1701 William Penn signed the **Charter of Privileges,** a document that, among other things, granted religious freedom (so long as there was a belief in God) in his colony of Pennsylvania. Because of this right, over a dozen sects of Christianity were celebrated in Philadelphia. Catholics were in the minority when they built their first two

The understated original entrance to Old St. Mary's church reflects a time when Catholicism was not widely practiced in Philadelphia.

churches, St. Joseph's in 1733 and St. Mary's in 1763. That was a step ahead of New York and Boston; those cities didn't have Roman Catholic churches until after the American Revolution.

Although the main entrance of St. Mary's now fronts right onto the sidewalk of 4th Street, it originally was located on 5th Street, in a more discreet setting separated from the thoroughfare by the churchyard. This placement reflected an acknowledgment of Roman Catholicism's lower perceived place among the Christian religions in town. Despite initial prejudices to Catholics, in 1779 the church hosted the first public religious celebration to mark the signing of the Declaration of Independence three years earlier. In a show of unity, members of the Continental Congress attended this service.

The cemetery opened in 1759, a few years before the church, with bodies transferred from the Catholic section of the burial ground in Washington Square. It received a huge influx of corpses during the yellow fever epidemic of 1793. Among the more than 5,000 deaths during the affliction, over 350 were Catholics. During the two months marking the height of the epidemic, September and October, there were over 300 funerals at St. Mary's.

The prominent people buried at Old St. Mary's include **John Barry,** the "Father of the United States Navy"; **Thomas Fitzsimons,** one of only two Catholic delegates to the Constitutional Convention of 1787; and **Michel Bouvier,** the great-great-grandfather of **Jacqueline Bouvier Kennedy Onassis.** Bouvier was a cabinetmaker who fled France after Napoleon was defeated in 1815 and created a real-estate empire in Philadelphia. His circa-1850 Italianate home at 260 S. 3rd St., just a block east of Old St. Mary's, sold for $2.5 million in 2012.

Despite the negative perception that some colonists had of St. Mary's papal influence, in a show of unity George Washington and John Adams each attended Sunday Mass here on at least one occasion.

John Barry: The Father of the United States Navy

A statue of Commodore John Barry pointing robustly into the distance occupies a commanding position in Independence Square, yet most visitors have not heard of this Revolutionary figure. Let's learn a little about Commodore John Barry. He . . .

. . . was born in Wexford, Ireland, in 1745 to poor tenant farmers.

. . . grew up in the Philadelphia area with a love of sailing on the Delaware River and became a merchant ship captain.

. . . could look down on the formidable George Washington, at 6 feet, 4 inches tall.

. . . captured the first British ship of the war in April 1776.

. . . fought in the last naval battle of the war off the coast of Cape Canaveral, Florida.

. . . captained the ship that returned the Marquis de Lafayette to France after the war.

. . . was personally awarded Commission Number One in the new United States Navy by President George Washington in 1797.

. . . along with John Paul Jones is considered the Father of the United States Navy.

. . . is honored with the Commodore Barry Bridge which links Pennsylvania and South Jersey.

. . . died in Philadelphia on September 13, 1803, at the age of 58 and is buried at Old St. Mary's Church.

The latter was quite affected by it and penned a note to Abigail about the Mass, observing, "The music, consisting of an organ and a choir of singers, went all the afternoon except sermon time, and the assembly chanted most sweetly and exquisitely. Here is everything which can lay hold of the eye, ear, and imagination—everything which can charm and bewitch the simple and ignorant. I wonder how Luther ever broke the spell." The interior of the church was remodeled in the 1970s, so it is not original.

```
Old St. Mary's Church and Churchyard Information

Location: 252 S. 4th St.

Hours: Mass is at 4:30 p.m. Sat and 10 a.m. Sun

Admission: Free

Phone: (215) 923-7930

Website: oldstmary.com

Wheelchair accessibility: One step to enter the church. Grave-
yard not wheelchair accessible.
```

Side Trip: Wistar House

Just north of St. Mary's, notice the **Wistar House** at 238 S. 4th St. It was built in 1750 as part of a group of homes called Surgeon's Row. Since colonial times Philadelphia has been on the cutting edge of medical care in the US. The house was first owned by Dr. William Shippen. Although he may be more known for being the uncle of Benedict Arnold's wife Peggy Shippen, he was instrumental in the development of the University of Pennsylvania's medical school. In 1798 Dr. Caspar Wistar moved into the residence where he aided the success of the **Lewis & Clark Expedition;** he hosted Meriwether Lewis in Philadelphia and trained him in anatomy and paleontology for his upcoming journey. The Wistar house went on the market in 2014 with an asking price of $2,750,000, but hey, it does come with three parking spaces.

Side Trip: Old St. Joseph's

Continue north on 4th Street for a half-block until you get to Willings Alley and look for a wooden sign that says Old St. Joseph's National Shrine at 321 Willings Alley. Jesuit priests built a chapel on the site in 1733, making it the first Roman Catholic church in Philadelphia. It was not without controversy as some opposed the creation of a religious institution with "Mass openly celebrated by a Popish priest contrary to the laws of England." Eventually the Provincial Council ruled that the Charter of Privileges that created Pennsylvania and granted religious freedom overruled any objections to the church. The current Gothic brick structure was erected in 1839. Don't be fooled by its simple façade. It's worth popping your head in to view the beautiful sanctuary. The interior has undergone some changes over the years, but the striking altar with double ionic columns is original, as is the crucifixion painting by Sylvano Martinez based on an etching by Peter Paul Rubens.

Pit Stop: Rose Garden and Magnolia Garden

On Locust Street between 4th and 5th Streets you'll find two small gardens that are a relatively unknown part of Independence National Historical Park. These spaces were set aside to form a natural "green" connection between the Park and the historic Society Hill neighborhood to the south. They each provide a respite for aching feet.

On the north side of Locust Street lies the **Rose Garden,** so named for more than 200 rose bushes planted by the Daughters of the American Revolution to honor the signers of the Declaration of Independence. There are 56 varieties of heirloom roses, one for each signer; each variety existed during the time of the Revolution.

Colonial-style brick walls enclose the garden; rooftops and church spires of nearby 18th-century buildings are visible through shade trees lining the border. The roses take center stage in the sun, offering a kaleidoscope of color in summer. The garden's northern entrance (off Walnut Street) was once the courtyard for a stable; notice the cobblestones, which date from about 1796. Several benches line the brick walkways in both shady and sunny spots offering a quiet place to stop and (you knew this was coming) smell the roses.

If you fancy the sound of trickling water in your gardens, head south across Locust Street and pass through the wrought-iron gates to the smaller **Magnolia Garden.** Designated as a "tribute" garden honoring the nation's founders, it was donated by the Garden Club of America. Inspiration for the design was George Washington's interest in magnolia trees: 13 of them are planted around the perimeter, one for each of the original colonies.

The garden is an oval of lawn surrounded by a walking path and white iron benches. A fountain produces a soothing trickle that offsets the surrounding city noises. This tiny green pocket is pretty all year, but visit in spring to see the magnolias blooming in all their pink and white glory, or early summer when an abundance of white azaleas punctuates the green.

Both the **Rose Garden** and **Magnolia Garden** are located mid-block on Locust Street between 4th and 5th Streets and are open daily from 9 a.m. to 5 p.m. *Note:* The Rose Garden has an additional entrance on Walnut Street between 4th and 5th Streets.

Powel House
224 South 3rd Street

The four-story brick Powel House, reminiscent of a London townhome, was where virtually "anyone who was anyone" came to socialize and discuss the issues of the day, before, during, and after the Revolution.

The home was built in 1766 by Scotsman Charles Stedman, a prosperous Philadelphia merchant and iron magnate. A few years later, the upwardly mobile **Samuel Powel III,** the young heir to a sprawling real-estate empire at age 18, purchased it.

Returning to Philadelphia from a seven-year Grand Tour of Europe, Powel put on his big boy britches and purchased the home in 1769, five days before his marriage to **Elizabeth Willing.** After moving in he upgraded an already formidable home.

Some of the finest carvers and craftsmen in the colonies plied their trade in Philadelphia, several of whom hung their tool belts at

the Powel house for the duration of the home's extreme makeover. The architectural woodwork they created is a fine example of the Rococo style that jazzed up Georgian interiors, as well as adding decorative motifs in papier mâché that was molded into an almost infinite array of shapes. Some of the work was contracted to Robert Smith, the carpenter-builder whose name pops up so much in early Philadelphia that one wonders if he had several competitors with the same name.

The dining room is considered the first of its kind in Philadelphia. Of course, people dined in their homes before, but they did so in multipurpose rooms. During his Grand Tour of Europe Powel visited palatial homes with dedicated dining rooms and brought the exotic concept to Philadelphia. The pretzel-back Chippendale chairs on display are original to the home. **George Washington** admired them so much he had two dozen crafted for Mount Vernon.

Grand entrance to the Powel House.

The second-floor back parlor and ballroom were particularly orna-
mented, done up in filigreed plasterwork including ornate leaf-and-scroll
carving taken right out of Swan's *Designs in Architecture*, the trend-setting
London book that was all the rage in the mid-18th century. However,
to gaze upon the original parlor you'll have to go to New York's Metro-
politan Museum of Art, and to pirouette through the original ballroom

---

A Close Shave

The apothecary scale in the front parlor of the Powel House was
a gift from Benjamin Franklin. Tenants paid their rent to Powel
in coins, but the coins were often shaved around the edges and
the precious metal reused elsewhere. When Powel weighed the
coins he knew if he was receiving fair value. Eventually coins
were marked with serrated edges to hamper this practice, just
like that quarter in your pocket.

---

you'll need to head across town to the Philadelphia Museum of Art. In the early 20th century the Powel House was a warehouse for a company importing horsehair from Siberia. To raise some money the owner sold

The reproduced ornate ballroom where George and Martha Washington danced.

the interiors to the respective museums. The building was in such a state of neglect that this action likely saved the interiors from destruction.

The Powels were known for their grand hospitality and the mansion was a de rigueur stop in the capital city's budding social circuit. Among the frequent guests were **Dr. Benjamin Rush** and **John Adams.** The fine hospitality impressed **George and Martha Washington** so much they were frequent guests of the Powel's and even celebrated their 20th wedding anniversary with a fête in the ornate ballroom.

Powel House Information

Location: 224 South 3rd Street

Hours: 12 to 4 p.m. Thurs through Sat, 1 p.m. to 4 p.m. Sun, Feb 25 through Dec 31; by appointment only Jan 1 through Feb 28

Admission: Adults, $8; seniors and students, $6; $20 per family; free to members and those 6 and under

Phone: (215) 627-0364

Website: philalandmarks.org

Wheelchair accessibility: Not wheelchair accessible.

Samuel Powel was the last mayor of Philadelphia before the Revolution, and mayor again after the British were defeated, earning him the nickname the **"Patriot Mayor."** He was also one of the pallbearers at Benjamin Franklin's funeral. Three years after Franklin's death Powel joined him in eternity, one of the many victims of the yellow fever epidemic of 1793. His name lives on in Powelton Village, a neighborhood of Victorian homes adjacent to the Drexel University campus in West Philadelphia, near the Powel family summer estate that overlooked the Schuylkill River.

Side Trip: A Royal Paine

One of the biggest spurs urging the colonies into open rebellion was the writing of **Thomas Paine**. A blue-and-yellow Pennsylvania Historical Marker at the southeast corner of 3rd and Thomas Paine Place (Chancellor Street) marks the spot where **Robert Bell** printed the first edition of Paine's *Common Sense* in January 1776. A native Englishman, Paine arrived in Philadelphia in 1774 with a letter of recommendation from Benjamin Franklin tucked into his sleeve. In early 1775 he put his literary skills to good use writing about a variety of topics for *The Pennsylvania Magazine*.

By the end of that pivotal year he was off on his own, writing a pamphlet called *Common Sense*. Paine wrote forcefully about the foolishness of the monarchy. He thought it absurd that someone could rule over people merely because they inherited a title, and attacked the very logic of such a system of government.

Paine's incendiary 79-page pamphlet had a huge impact on the tide of public opinion and became a bestseller, igniting a political firestorm throughout the colonies. Perhaps his pen wasn't mightier than the sword, but his ideas caused many swords to be sharpened for the impending war.

Life During Wartime

It wasn't all silk and soirees among the gentry in colonial Philadelphia. The road to the American Revolution increased the strategic importance of the city, making it a natural target for occupation by the British army, who settled in for nine months starting on September 26, 1777.

Life during the occupation was harsh. The immediate worry was a spike in prices for coffee, flour, and other goods—that is, when they were even available. Tea, that essential British cure-all for any type of adversity, sold for $60 per pound. Quaker **Elizabeth Sandwith Drinker** recorded in her diary, "the Hessians go on plundering at a great rate; such things as wood, potatoes, turnips. Provisions are scarce among us." A few days later a British soldier, with much apology and blaming it on General Howe's orders, confiscated one of her remaining blankets. By December, wooden fencing was being torn down for firewood and in her listing of food prices Drinker comments on the going rate for rats in the countryside. Yes, *rats!*

The British commander, **General Howe,** no slouch in the comfort department, requisitioned the mansion of former governor Richard Penn. (This home on Market Street was later the residence of George Washington when he was president.) He seemed content with his cozy existence in Philadelphia and was in no hurry to disrupt the colonial troops, who were quite vulnerable in their winter encampment only 20 miles to the west at Valley Forge. When Benjamin Franklin, then living in Paris, heard about Howe's occupation of Philadelphia he observed that on the contrary, Philadelphia had taken Howe.

The lack of supplies didn't prevent the British from staging a bustling social scene. The most extravagant fête was called the **Meschianza,** a grand bash organized by **Major John André** (the spy who was later hanged for his role in the conspiracy with Benedict Arnold to hand over West Point to the British) that happened on May 18, 1778, to honor the departing General Howe. Along with the parade of ships and fireworks on the river, it even included a jousting tournament; the British officers wore medieval costumes while their comely dates dressed as exotic Turkish maidens. Elizabeth Drinker's reaction to the party probably spoke for many in Philadelphia: "How insensible do these people appear, while our Land is so greatly desolated, and Death and sore destruction has overtaken, and now impends, over so many!"

By the time the British army abandoned Philadelphia and left for New York the next month, they had a gaggle of about 3,000 loyalists straggling along who feared retribution when the Continental Army moved back into the capital city.

Mr. and Mrs. Powel walked a fine line, being neither ardent Revolutionaries nor Tories. Despite being the mayor of the city, Samuel Powel was still a politician and tried not to offend either constituency. The couple stayed in the city alongside the British, but after their home was requisitioned by the Earl of Carlisle, who moved into the main quarters, the Powels were shunted into the rear servant's section of the building. Powel's hedging of his bets on the Revolution paid off; after the war ended he was once again elected mayor of Philadelphia.

Carpenters' Court

Many of the sights in this section are part of Independence National Historical Park, yet are often overlooked by tourists. The buildings here help bring to life the political (and social) maneuverings that took place in the years before and after the signing of the Declaration of Independence.

Visit **Carpenters' Hall,** where the First Continental Congress met in 1774 and contemplated the radical idea of breaking away from England; explore the massive Greek Revival bank buildings that helped give Philadelphia the nickname the "Athens of America"; and learn about conflicts within the new government that led to the creation—and ultimate demise—of those banks.

There may still be a spark of romance at the **Dolley Todd Madison House,** where one of American politics' first "power couples" met. In the small parlor James Madison, a dashing (or at least very eligible), congressman from Virginia courted a young widow named Dolley. Sparks of a more political bent flew in the drinking rooms at **City Tavern,** where revolutionary ideas were debated over a pint or two.

If that doesn't paint a true enough picture of colonial Philadelphia, take a peek at the **Portrait Gallery at the Second Bank of the United States** to put some faces to all those famous names. And don't worry, it's more interesting than it sounds; even children will get the picture.

Dolley Todd Madison House
Northeast corner of 4th and Walnut Streets

This circa-1775 three-story brick residence is named after **Dolley Todd Madison,** who lived here with her first husband John Todd, a

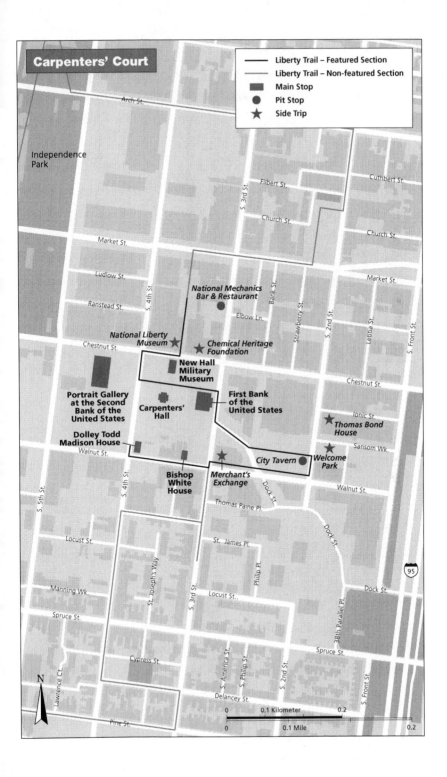

Carpenters' Court

Legend:
- Liberty Trail – Featured Section
- Liberty Trail – Non-featured Section
- Main Stop
- Pit Stop
- Side Trip

Independence Park

Arch St.

Filbert St.

Cuthbert St.

S. 3rd St.

Church St.

Church St.

Market St.

Ludlow St.

Market St.

Ranstead St.

S. 4th St.

National Mechanics Bar & Restaurant

Elbow Ln.

Bank St.

Strawberry St.

S. 2nd St.

Letitia St.

S. Front St.

National Liberty Museum

Chestnut St.

Chemical Heritage Foundation

New Hall Military Museum

Chestnut St.

Portrait Gallery at the Second Bank of the United States

Carpenters' Hall

First Bank of the United States

Ionic St.

Thomas Bond House

Dolley Todd Madison House

Walnut St.

S. 4th St.

Bishop White House

Merchant's Exchange

City Tavern

Sansom Wk.

Welcome Park

Walnut St.

Thomas Paine Pl.

Dock St.

S. 5th St.

Locust St.

St. James Pl.

Philip Pl.

Dock St.

95

Manning Wk.

St. Joseph's Way

S. 3rd St.

Locust St.

38th Parallel Pl.

Dock St.

Spruce St.

Spruce St.

S. Front St.

Cypress St.

S. America St.

S. Philip St.

S. 2nd St.

N

Lawrence Ct.

Delancey St.

Pine St.

0   0.1 Kilometer   0.2

0   0.1 Mile   0.2

The house is on the corner for added light and ventilation. The doorway to the right is for the adjacent townhouse.

lawyer who died in the yellow fever epidemic of 1793. The building is officially known as the Todd House, but it's become more popular to refer to it by the more recognizable Madison name, after Dolley's second husband, **James Madison.**

With its plain white walls and simple furnishings, the home reflects its owner's Quaker beliefs and is more subdued than the elegantly decorated Bishop White House a few doors down on Walnut Street. The two houses should be toured together to give the visitor a contrasting view of everyday life in late 18th-century Philadelphia.

The ground floor consists mostly of the kitchen and dining room, reflecting the importance of those mealtimes in daily life, with one room set aside for Todd's legal practice. The kitchen displays common implements that were used in the 1790s. The home's corner setting presents a grander appearance than most townhouses, with a longer façade along 4th Street. Despite the stately exterior, unlike their wealthier neighbors the Whites, the Todds had to go outside to take care of their personal hygiene in a public privy, a common practice of the time.

Dolley and John Todd were married for only three years when a yellow fever epidemic hit Philadelphia in 1793. The breadth of devastation was conveyed in a letter Thomas Jefferson wrote in September 1793: "An infectious and deadly fever has broken out in this place. The deaths under it, during the week before last, were about forty, the last week fifty, and this week I fear they will be two hundred, so rapidly is it increasing. Everyone is leaving the city who can."

Todd felt a duty to his law clients to remain in the city and help them prepare their wills while his young wife and two small children fled to Gray's Ferry, a community on the Schuylkill River just a short distance away. Within days both Dolley's husband and three-week-old child succumbed to the raging fever. Dolley was also infected and fought for weeks until she recovered.

After her husband's death, Dolley Todd was a 25-year-old widow with a small boy to support. In those times it was not uncommon for widows to take up right away with a new beau. Dolley shortly met Virginia Congressman **James Madison.** The two were introduced by Senator **Aaron Burr,** years before he gained notoriety as Thomas Jefferson's vice president. Some say Dolley and Madison courted in the second-floor parlor room.

When Dolley wed Madison she was expelled from the Quaker church for marrying someone outside the faith. She also moved out of her Walnut Street home; from 1794 to 1797 the newlyweds lived in Madison's more elegant mansion on Spruce Street.

Despite the Quakers' disapproval of her new husband, she did pretty well for herself; Madison eventually became the fourth president of the United States.

Bishop White House
309 Walnut Street

Bishop William White was the longtime rector of both **Christ Church** and **St. Peter's Church** and the first Episcopal bishop of Pennsylvania. He was pro-revolution, but wielded a moderating influence, working diligently on the difficult balancing act of keeping the American church united while not severing ties with the Church of England. Reflecting his beliefs in the cause of independence, he served as the Chaplain for the **Continental Congress** from 1777 to 1789.

White moved into his newly built house in 1787 and lived there along with, at various times, a dozen children and grandchildren, until his death in 1836. The home is located midway between his two churches, providing a convenient starting point for his daily commute. It was built after the Revolutionary War so the architectural style is no longer considered Georgian, a name that reflects an homage to King George, but federal, signifying the importance of the new nation and its burgeoning native tastes in art, furniture, and architecture.

Exterior of the Bishop White House with federal-style doorway.

During the yellow fever epidemic of 1793 friends urged White to leave town, but he remained in the city to offer spiritual aid to those afflicted by the disease. He may have survived due to the sophisticated mosquito netting he had draped around his bed. At the time it wasn't yet known that mosquitoes spread the disease, so he may have lucked out.

White lived in the house with his wife Mary, who was the daughter of a former mayor of Philadelphia. The house is decorated as it was for an upper-class gentleman of his day, which, despite his religious vocation, White most certainly was. The Canton porcelain that graces the tables and fine antique furniture are originals, preserved by his granddaughters.

The bishop traveled in formidable social circles. His brother-in-law was **Robert Morris,** one of the financiers of the American Revolution, and a next-door neighbor was the most famous doctor in the city, **Dr. Benjamin Rush.** One sign of White's relative wealth is the **indoor privy,** quite the luxury at the time.

However, the creek behind the house carried the waste from emptying all those indoor privy pots, along with runoff from local tanneries, creating a foul stench (and was likely a source of the mosquitoes that spread the fatal yellow fever).

Tours of the Bishop White House are offered in conjunction with the adjacent Todd House.

Bishop White House Information

Location: 309 Walnut St.

Hours: Periodically closed due to federal budget cuts. Check the website for current schedule.

Admission: Free. Tickets are available at the Independence Visitor Center.

Phone: (215) 965-2305

Website: nps.gov/inde/bishop-white-house.htm

Wheelchair accessibility: Portable ramp can be placed over steps when requested.

Side Trip: Merchants' Exchange Building

Across 3rd Street from the Bishop White House stands the **Merchants' Exchange Building** (143 S. 3rd St.), yet another of architect William Strickland's Greek Revival masterpieces. His work is on display at the Second Bank of the United States and the National Mechanics restaurant and pops up again here. The 1834 structure was unusual from the get-go; due to the curve of Dock Street it's the rare building in Philadelphia that was designed for a triangle-shaped lot. The cobblestoned street coursing in front of it used to be Dock Creek before it was paved over. When viewed

A touch of ancient Greece in Philadelphia.

from the west the building displays a typical monumental Greek Revival face. But saunter around to the opposite side for a different perspective; the unusual shape of the lot led to the semi-circular Corinthian-columned portico on the eastern façade, giving the building a unique character that sticks out like a marble thumb in this section of the historic district that is dominated by brick.

The lantern tower on the top floor, based on the Monument of Lysicrates in ancient Greece, helped Philadelphia live up to its early 19th-century title **"the Athens of America."** It also served a dual purpose; merchants climbed up to the tower to view the arrivals of their ships on the Delaware River.

The National Park Service acquired the structure in 1952 and it now houses their offices. The lobby, where you can view displays about the building and the area, is open Mon through Fri from 8 a.m. to 4:30 p.m.

Pit Stop: City Tavern

If the Founding Fathers had been teetotalers perhaps the American Revolution might never have happened. As it turns out, they liked to imbibe a tankard of ale or a glass of Madeira now and then and the place to do it was the bustling **City Tavern** (138 S. 2nd St., 215-413-1443).

Established in 1773, it was also known as Smith's Tavern, after its manager Daniel Smith. During the British occupation of Philadelphia that began in September 1777, Smith turned out to be a loyalist. When the British army abandoned town and headed for New York nine months later, he skedaddled along with them in order to avoid reprisals from the returning Continental Army. That explains why City Tavern is no longer known as Smith's Tavern. To the victor go the spoils, or in this case, the naming rights.

The re-created City Tavern is a congenial rest stop on the Philadelphia Liberty Trail.

Did you say you want a revolution? The second-floor Long Room at City Tavern helped launch independence.

Government affairs and the latest hot-button political issues were fiercely debated in this public gathering spot, making it the place where the rabble started to rouse. Patrons tarried in the first-floor coffee room to catch up on the latest news from American and British newspapers on the festering relationship with the mother country. The **Long Room** on the second floor was the initial meeting place for delegates to the **First Continental Congress** in 1774 before they selected Carpenters' Hall as their home, so it can be said that the notion of liberty was first openly discussed in the ale-soaked rooms of City Tavern.

Lobster Again?

The supply of lobsters was in such abundance in colonial America that it was known as "poor man's food." Some servants got so tired of eating it they asked that their ration of lobster be limited to three times a week.

When **John Adams** visited Philadelphia for the First Continental Congress he reported on political dinners at City Tavern with 100 guests in their prim buckled shoes sharing the latest gossip of the potential break from the mother country; it's perhaps one of the first "smoke-filled rooms" of political maneuvering. A sure sign that this was *the* hotbed of political discourse, when dispatch rider **Paul Revere** galloped into town during the 1774 Continental Congress with the latest news from seething Boston, he dropped off the messages at City Tavern. Revere pulled up to the tavern again the following spring with shocking reports of the gunfire at Lexington and Concord.

The original City Tavern was torn down in 1854 and accurately rebuilt on the site in time for the Bicentennial. Today City Tavern welcomes weary (or hungry) travelers for a meal served in an elegant colonial atmosphere. Although the building is owned by the National Park Service, the restaurant, run by award-winning chef Walter Staib, serves up authentic gourmet renditions of early American cuisine including lobster, turkey potpie, and even fried tofu from **Benjamin Franklin's** recipe; the Founding Father and gourmand experimented with being a vegetarian for a time in his early years. For more information on City Tavern see the **Where to Eat** section or go to citytavern.com.

Side Trip: Welcome Park

> William Penn was the greatest lawgiver the world has produced. Being the first either in ancient or modern times who has laid the foundation of government in the pure and unadulterated principles of peace, reason, and right.
>
> —*Thomas Jefferson, 1825*

Look for the statue of **William Penn** located diagonally to the left across the street from City Tavern. It sits in the middle of **Welcome Park,** a 24/7 outdoor museum that's a must stop for map geeks and those who'd like to get a bit of perspective on William Penn's trendsetting plan for Philadelphia. Named after the ship that William Penn sailed to America on his first visit in 1682, Welcome Park provides an urban escape in the historic district.

The park is located on the site of William Penn's Slate Roof House, where Penn lived from 1699 to 1701. Despite the incredible and irreplaceable history it represented, the house was torn down in 1867. Welcome Park opened on the tricentennial of William Penn first setting foot in Philadelphia.

Penn only lived in his colony from 1682 to 1684 and from 1699 to 1701. When he returned to England he suffered some business setbacks, which landed him a stint in a debtor's prison. In 1712 he suffered a stroke and his wife, **Hannah Callowhill Penn,** became the acting governor of

Welcome Park is set on a grid highlighting Penn's original plan for Philadelphia. City Tavern peeks through the trees on the far side.

The Curse of Billy Penn

Despite his pacifist Quaker beliefs, Penn was a man to be reckoned with, even 300 years after founding his colony. When the Philadelphia 76ers won the NBA title in 1983, it marked the end of a golden era for Philadelphia sports teams. They entered a drought of winning seasons, their champs turning to chumps. And the man they had to thank for it was none other than the city's founding father, William Penn. The reason? His spirit was apparently miffed about being eclipsed.

According to a "gentleman's agreement," no building in Philadelphia could be taller than the brim of Penn's hat on the massive statue of him (designed by **Alexander Milne Calder**) that stands atop City Hall. No building broke this agreement until 1987 when the 61-story One Liberty Place overshadowed Penn's likeness. Around that time Philly sports teams went into a swoon. Soon three more buildings joined One Liberty Place in breaking the previous height limit. A few sharp fans caught on to the connection and the **"Curse of Billy Penn"** was born.

In 2007 Comcast was completing construction of a new headquarters in Center City Philadelphia that dwarfed all previous skyscrapers. (It's the silver building at 17th Street and JFK Boulevard that looks like a giant flash drive.) At the topping-out ceremony, a miniature replica of the Billy Penn statue was attached to the iron beam that was hoisted almost 1,000 feet into the sky. Penn was back where he belonged, looking down on his "greene country towne."

And then a funny thing happened. That year the Phillies made the playoffs with an unexpected late-season winning streak. The next year they won the World Series, the first title for the city since the brim of Penn's hat was surpassed in height. The curse of Billy Penn was broken and all was well with the world . . . or at least with Philadelphia.

the Pennsylvania colony. After he died in 1718 he was laid to rest in a Quaker burial ground in the village of Chalfont St. Giles, on the outskirts of London.

You have to look down at your feet to view the key feature of the park; the trend-setting geometrical city plan is laid out in marble tiles at ground level. The squares that Penn set aside for green space are planted with trees. In the middle is a smaller version of the William Penn statue that stands tall atop Philadelphia's City Hall at Center Square. A model of Penn's Slate Roof House sits on the map where it originally existed.

Lining the outdoor walls of this Lilliputian version of Philadelphia are vignettes from Penn's life, including the time he was kicked out of Oxford for holding religious services in his room rather than attending chapel.

The brick building overlooking the park on the north side is the **Thomas Bond House,** a genteel bed-and-breakfast in the former home of Thomas Bond, one of the founders, along with Benjamin Franklin, of Pennsylvania Hospital, and yes, since this is Philadelphia, it was America's first hospital. (For more about the Thomas Bond House, turn to the **Where to Stay** section of this book.)

If you're traveling with kids who need to burn off some energy, then Welcome Park offers some relief. They'll love running around the open space and making a game of staying within the city streets on the ground-level map.

First Bank of the United States
116 South 3rd Street

The **First Bank of the United States** is significant for its cutting-edge architecture, but even more so for the activities that occurred within the building. The bank symbolized a new country making its debut on the international stage, longing to be taken seriously by more established nations.

After the United States gained its independence it struggled financially. It lacked a uniform currency; each colony issued its own form of

Classical architecture comes to America.

money. The country had incurred huge debts to support the war but lacked an efficient means of paying them off. A central bank would address these issues while encouraging commercial loans to fund merchant activity.

Alexander Hamilton was the first secretary of the treasury in 1790 when he proposed the creation of a national bank. It was chartered a year later. The government recognized the need for a formidable building that conveyed the solidity of the new nation's finances.

However, due to political infighting between northern and southern interests, Congress did not renew the bank's charter and it only operated from 1791 through 1811.

The building was designed by **Samuel Blodgett Jr.** He was not a professional architect but had wangled a job as the superintendent of buildings for the new Federal City being built along the Potomac

Across the street is the site of the proposed **Museum of the American Revolution,** which will focus on the years 1750 to 1800, covering the lead up to war and the founding of the new nation. Exhibits will include George Washington's campaign tent, silver camp cups from his field kit, and other artifacts. Further information on the museum is available at amrevmuseum.org.

River. (You may know it as Washington, D.C.) Like a proud peacock his building displayed all the bells and whistles of the neoclassical style, harkening back to ancient Greece, which was taking root in America.

In a first for an American building, the façade is clad in white marble. Note the portico and ornate 56-foot-high Corinthian columns gracing the front entrance, the first building in Philadelphia to be so decorated. In a nod to federalism the tympanum, the triangular space over the entry portico, is decorated with a carved wood American eagle, one of the first uses of the bird to represent America.

The interior of the building has been drastically altered over the years so no one is sure what the original looked like. It houses offices for the National Park Service and is not open to the public. But it's worth a gander to appreciate a preeminent example of early American neoclassical architecture in a building whose function kept the early United States financially afloat and ensured its survival.

First Bank of the United States Information

Location: 116 S. 3rd St.

Hours: Interior is closed to the public

Carpenters' Hall
320 Chestnut Street

Carpenters' Hall is nestled 200 feet off Chestnut Street, its façade barely visible behind the New Hall Military Museum and the Pemberton House. With all the modern development nearby, it's hard to imagine that when Carpenters' Hall was built in 1770 it was placed just outside the edge of the burgeoning city. Hidden it may be, but in some aspects Carpenters' Hall is every bit as important as Independence Hall, located 1 block west. While it's often overshadowed by Independence Hall, **Carpenters' Hall** was where the seeds of liberty were first planted.

The **First Continental Congress** met here on September 5, 1774, for a two-and-a-half-month session. It was the first time that men elected by the assemblies of 12 colonies (Georgia didn't participate) met to air their grievances against British rule. Delegates included

It's pastoral now, but Carpenters' Hall used to be crammed in among other buildings.
PHOTO COURTESY CHRIS ROBART

then-Colonel George Washington and John Adams. At the first session Patrick Henry reflected the new sense of unity taking place in the colonies when he declared, "The distinctions between Pennsylvanians, New Yorkers and New Englanders are no more. I am not a Virginian, but an American."

Founded in 1724, the **Carpenters' Company of the City and County of Philadelphia** is the oldest trade guild in America. The purpose of the organization was twofold: to provide instruction in architecture and to assist members, or their families, who needed financial help due to an accident. The guild also established a **"Book of Prices"** to value a carpenter's work. The group was set up along similar lines to the Worshipful Company of Carpenters, which was founded in London in 1477. The Carpenters' Company is still an active organization with members from the building, architectural, and engineering fields.

The guild selected **Robert Smith,** a Scottish-trained carpenter-architect, to design a headquarters building. He sketched out a 50-foot-tall red-brick building with cutouts at the corners, giving it the appearance from a Google satellite's-eye view of a symmetrical Greek cross, the better to allow in more light.

Its weight is supported by 13-inch-thick walls with the bricks set in a Flemish bond pattern, a strong system where stretcher bricks are laid out lengthwise and alternated with header bricks where only the short end is visible. At Carpenters' Hall the headers are darker, the result of being smoked in the manufacturing process, to create an orderly checkerboard effect. The rounded Palladian windows on the second floor of the north façade impart a refined air such as was found in the finest buildings in London. The two-story brick structure represents a high point of Georgian style architecture.

Carpenters' Hall was a popular place to rent space, becoming an incubator for up-and-coming institutions; the American Philosophical Society and the Library Company of Philadelphia were among the early tenants. It's also considered the site of the first Library of Congress; when the First Continental Congress met here several members climbed up the stairs to the second floor Library Company to peruse the selection and borrow books. During the occupation of Philadelphia by the British, Carpenters' Hall was converted, as many public buildings were, into a military hospital.

In 1857 the members of the company recognized the building's significance from both architectural and historical viewpoints, and withdrew it from commercial endeavors to focus on preserving its past. It was restored and reopened to the public, the first privately owned building in America that could be visited as a historic monument and a significant early step in the historic preservation movement.

Today the interior is furnished as it was during the First Continental Congress. One of the more popular items is a scale model that shows Carpenters' Hall under construction and reveals 18th-century building techniques. Do-it-yourselfers will appreciate the exhibit of antique carpentry tools on display in the entryway. Unlike Independence Hall, you can walk right in without a timed ticket and soak up the atmosphere. Carpenters' Hall looks its most majestic when it is approached from the

A model building.
PHOTO COURTESY CHRIS ROBART

America's First Dumbest Criminal

Philadelphia is a city of many firsts, so it shouldn't be surprising that the first bank robbery in America went down here. In 1798, Carpenters' Hall was leased to the Bank of Pennsylvania. One hot summer night it was robbed of $162,821 (over $3.5 million today). Suspicion immediately fell on **Patrick Lyon,** a blacksmith who had supplied the new vault doors and locks. He was arrested and tossed into Walnut Street Prison. But in an act that could land him on an episode of *America's Dumbest Criminals,* a carpenter and member of the Company named **Isaac Davis,** who had actually pulled off the heist, deposited large sums of money into the very same bank he had just robbed. This raised a few eyebrows and he was arrested. Davis worked out a deal to return the stolen loot in exchange for not being charged, which left the unfortunate Lyon still languishing in jail. He spent three months there for a crime he did not commit, before the still-suspicious authorities released him.

Carpenters' Hall Information

Location: 320 Chestnut St.

Hours: Open daily, except Mon (and Tues in Jan and Feb), from 10 a.m. to 4 p.m.

Admission: Free

Phone: (215) 925-0167

Website: carpentershall.com

Wheelchair accessibility: The first floor is wheelchair accessible; restrooms are located on the second floor with only stairway access.

Note: Carpenters' Hall is part of Independence National Park but is still privately owned by the Carpenters' Company of the City and County of Philadelphia, as it has been since they built it in the 18th century.

rear via Harmony Street, a small walkway that can be accessed from either South 3rd or South 4th Streets.

New Hall Military Museum
320 Chestnut Street

The New Hall Military Museum is a reproduction of the original building on the site. The Carpenters' Company built the original New Hall for themselves in 1791 when they needed space after renting out Carpenters' Hall to the Bank of the United States. New Hall is sometimes referred to as the First Pentagon since the Carpenters' Company shared the building with the fledgling US War Department. Today it's hard to imagine the Department of Defense squeezing in with a trade guild, but in early America the War Department consisted of Secretary Henry Knox and a handful of employees.

The exterior of the New Hall Military Museum.

Exhibits highlight the early years of the army, navy and marines. Current and former leathernecks will enjoy the first-floor exhibit revealing the history of "Marines in the Revolution," while the upper floors are devoted to the nascent country's army and navy. The somewhat dated displays lean more heavily on static exhibits such as models of fighting ships and colonial-era muskets and cutlasses. One highlight is the *Raleigh*, the first American vessel to hoist the Stars-and-Stripes flag.

Just outside New Hall, military reenactors in historically accurate uniforms dramatically convey the moments of sheer terror during

New Hall Military Museum Information

Location: 320 Chestnut St., in front of Carpenters' Hall

Hours: The museum has been closed periodically due to federal budget cutbacks. Check nps.gov/inde/planyourvisit/hours.htm for the current schedule or call ahead.

Admission: Free

Phone: (215) 965-2305

Website: nps.gov/inde/new-hall.htm

Wheelchair accessibility: A portable ramp can be placed over the steps when requested.

pitched battles with the redcoats that punctuated the dreary, lonely, and often bitterly cold life of a soldier during the Revolution.

Pit Stop: European Republic

One block east of the New Hall Military Museum is **European Republic** (213 Chestnut St.). This bite-sized casual cafe offers healthy wrap sandwiches along with authentic European-style *frites* (freshly made french fries) with over 20 different toppings, ranging from mango chutney to roasted garlic to peanut sauce. Don't worry, though—for traditionalists they even have ketchup.

Portrait Gallery at the Second Bank of the United States
420 Chestnut Street

If the Second Bank of the United States looks a tad familiar, perhaps you've ventured to Athens, Greece, and viewed the Parthenon, the model for architect **William Strickland's** design. In fact, the bank's directors requested that the design be "a chaste imitation of Grecian architecture, in its simplest and least expensive form." Strickland won the commission after an intense competition that involved elite architects designing in the **Greek Revival style** that was sweeping the nation. When the building opened in 1824 it was an instant critical success. Today it houses the portrait collection of Independence Park and is worth visiting for both its sumptuous architecture and fine artwork.

If the US already had a Bank of the United States why did they need another one? In 1811 Congress declined to renew the charter for the **First Bank of the United States** and allowed it to wither away. Without its central guiding hand the states went back to issuing their own separate currencies and the financial system became muddled yet again. Along came the **War of 1812,** and the lack of a central bank made it difficult for the United States to borrow the needed funds to fight the British. Congress decided that perhaps a national bank wasn't

Philadelphia wasn't just a brick town anymore.
PHOTO COURTESY CHRIS ROBART

such a bad idea after all and in 1816 created the **Second Bank of the United States.**

Philadelphia financier **Nicholas Biddle** (his country estate **Andalusia** is listed in the **Farther Afield** section of this book) ran the bank and transformed it into a successful enterprise that built confidence in the nation's banking system. But once again politics intervened. In 1832 President Andrew Jackson vetoed the bill to renew the bank's charter, setting a precedent for the mighty power of the presidential pen.

Step inside to view the unexpected lemon-chiffon-colored barrel-vaulted ceiling and the walls painted in a bright pink hue, which can best be described as Early American Pepto-Bismol, providing a bright setting for the Portrait Gallery of Independence National Historical Park nestled within. The **"People of Independence"** exhibit showcases 185 paintings of colonial and federal figures. **George Washington,**

Thomas Jefferson, Benjamin Franklin, John Paul Jones, and **James and Dolley Madison** highlight the notables of the day.

One of the more colorful paintings that stands out from its sober, suit-clad brethren is that of **Thayendanegea,** also known as Joseph Brant. He's a Mohawk war chief who sided with the British and fought against the Americans during the Revolution. Charles Willson Peale captured his image when Brant visited Philadelphia on a diplomatic mission in 1797.

Over half the works were painted by **Charles Willson Peale,** one of the most accomplished portrait artists of his era. (Although naturally gifted in the arts, he put down his brush during the Revolution and replaced it with a musket when he joined the Philadelphia militia and fought in the Battles of Trenton and Princeton.) Peale's portraits

George Washington stands tall in the Portrait Gallery.

Benjamin Franklin by David Rent Etter, after Charles Willson Peale after David Martin, 1835.

were originally displayed on the second floor of Independence Hall where a museum operated by the Peale family was open until it went bankrupt in 1842, 15 years after the artist's death.

The Greek Revival style exemplified in the Second Bank of the United States was copied by bank branches and state capitol buildings throughout the country as a symbol of sober business and government principles. As for the bank that started it all, after its charter wasn't renewed it closed its doors. It was converted to use as a US Customs House, a role it served for nearly a century before it was eventually taken over by the National Park Service.

Portrait Gallery Information

Location: 420 Chestnut St.

Hours: Open Wed through Sun, 11 a.m. to 5 p.m.

Admission: Free

Phone: (215) 965-2305

Website: nps.gov/inde/second-bank.htm

Wheelchair accessibility: Wheelchair-accessible ramp located on the west side of the building. The gallery level is reached via elevator. Accessible restrooms are located in the basement near the elevator.

Side Trip: National Liberty Museum and Chemical Heritage Foundation

As you leave Carpenters' Court you'll pass by two privately run museums. The **National Liberty Museum** (321 Chestnut St.) is "dedicated to preserving America's heritage of freedom by fostering good character, civic responsibility and respect for all people." It does so through an eclectic display of glass sculptures, religion-themed exhibits including "Voyage to Liberty through Faith," and the tales of freedom fighters throughout history including Winston Churchill, Gandhi, and Andrei Sakharov. Admission fee. For more information go to libertymuseum.org.

A few doors east enter the headquarters of the **Chemical Heritage Foundation** (315 Chestnut St.) in the circa-1865 First National Bank building. Take a left in the lobby to enter the museum. The foundation's mission is "to foster dialogue on science and technology in society." They do so through artfully arranged exhibits such as **Making Modernity** that focuses on how chemistry has touched everyone. From Bakelite transistor radios to how standardized colors affected manufacturing, the displays effectively relate chemistry to our daily lives. The museum is definitely of the "Please Don't Touch" variety and is geared more toward those who have already taken a chemistry class in school. Free admission. For more information go to: chemheritage.org.

Pit Stop: National Mechanics Bar and Restaurant

It's not often we recommend a restaurant both for the yummy food and its historic architecture, but we'll make an exception for National Mechanics Bar and Restaurant (22 S. 3rd St.). It was built in 1837 for the Mechanics' Bank based on a design by the hot architect of the day, William Strickland.

He kept himself so busy running around designing grand Greek Revival edifices like this one in quaint Philadelphia that it was said of him, "He found us living in a city of brick and he will leave us in a city of marble." Strickland's surviving local works include the Merchants' Exchange (143 S. 3rd St.), the circa-1828 steeple atop Independence Hall, and his magnum opus, the Second Bank of the United States (420 Chestnut St.).

But enough about architecture. This is a Pit Stop, so you're here for the food. The menu appeals to the little kid in all of us. While they offer healthy salads, they really hit their stride with back-to-the-nest comfort food, much of which is kid-friendly—think corn dogs and pita pizza.

A crowd favorite is the Frito Taco Extravaganza. Picture a full bag of Fritos split open on your plate. Now picture it topped with perfectly spiced chili and shredded Monterey Jack cheese. Now picture yourself eating it. Add the bread pudding with seasonal fruits for dessert and you just might be done sightseeing for the day. At night the restaurant takes on a clubby vibe as hoodie-clad hipsters line up at the bar gulping PBR out of the can. But during the day and early evening it's so respectable you can even bring your demure Aunt Tillie along. For more information visit nationalmechanics.com.

OLD CITY

In Old City visitors experience a cross-section of Philadelphia's evolution from a small riverfront settlement to a thriving city. This portion of the Philadelphia Liberty Trail is unique in that it is not predominantly comprised of National Park property or revitalized colonial neighborhoods. Old City is a blend of the historic, the charmingly quaint, the simply "old," and the new, a vital place where Philadelphia honors its past, yet still keeps pace with the times.

In the 18th century Old City wasn't just a neighborhood. It was *the city*, the center of the action. Shops, churches, homes, and warehouses huddled near the bustling wharves on the Delaware River. The audacious towering spire of **Christ Church,** for a time the tallest building in the colonies, defined the skyline that sailors spotted as they neared port.

Perched near the bustling wharves, everything a Philadelphian needed 250 years ago could be found here. Penn's plan for market stalls on 100-foot-wide High Street (now Market) provided an early American shopping center while Second Street was the major north-south thoroughfare. Prominent Rhode Island physician Solomon Drowne, who studied medicine in Philadelphia in the mid 1770s, described the atmosphere on Second Street: "The thundering of Coaches, Chariots, Chaises, Waggons, Dreys and the whole Fraternity of Noise, almost continuously assail our Ears." While you don't have to dodge chariots or chaises today, Second Street still hums with the vibe of 19th-century warehouses that have been converted to shops, galleries, and loft apartments. Some of Philadelphia's oldest streets intersect it, including narrow **Elfreth's Alley,** inviting visitors to take a step back in time.

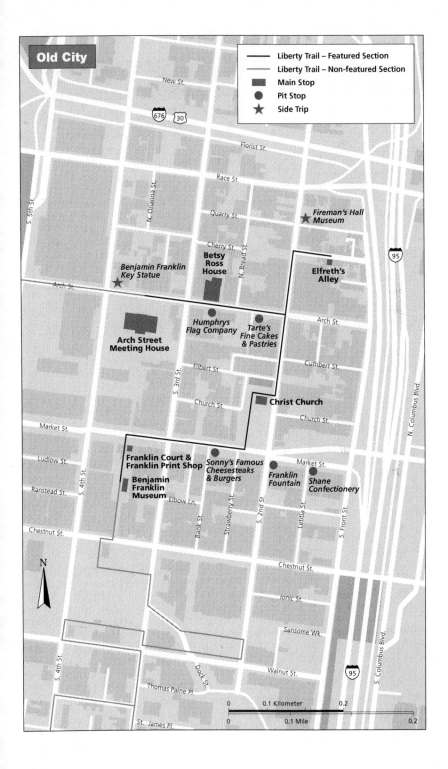

Old City

Liberty Trail – Featured Section
Liberty Trail – Non-featured Section
■ Main Stop
● Pit Stop
★ Side Trip

676 30

95

New St.

Florist St.

Race St.

Quarry St.

★ Fireman's Hall Museum

Cherry St.

Betsy Ross House

Benjamin Franklin Key Statue ★

Elfreth's Alley

Arch St.

Arch St.

● Humphrys Flag Company

● Tarte's Fine Cakes & Pastries

Arch Street Meeting House

Filbert St.

Cuthbert St.

S. 3rd St.

Church St.

■ Christ Church

Church St.

Market St.

Ludlow St.

Franklin Court & Franklin Print Shop

Sonny's Famous Cheesesteaks & Burgers

Market St.

● Franklin Fountain

● Shane Confectionery

Ranstead St.

Benjamin Franklin Museum

Elbow Ln.

Bank St.

Strawberry St.

S. 2nd St.

Letitia St.

S. Front St.

Chestnut St.

N. Columbus Blvd.

N

Chestnut St.

Ionic St.

Sansome Wk.

S. 4th St.

S. Columbus Blvd.

Dock St.

Walnut St.

95

Thomas Paine Pl.

| 0 | 0.1 Kilometer | 0.2 |

| 0 | 0.1 Mile | 0.2 |

St. James Pl.

The steeple of Christ Church blends in with funky Old City.

Merchants living over their shops was a tradition in the neighborhood, a way of life that's on view in the diminutive **Betsy Ross House,** where the young widow made curtains, chair cushions—and more than a few flags. According to longstanding legend she may have even sewn the first American flag.

Market Street has always been Philadelphia's commercial spine. The market stalls that once filled its center island are long gone, but the street remains a busy thoroughfare. Today it's lined with shops, restaurants, and **Franklin Court,** home to the **Benjamin Franklin Museum** and a ghostly "replica" of the inventor/printer/diplomat and all-around wit's house.

Explore Old City as you follow the Philadelphia Liberty Trail. You'll see how three centuries of a city can blend together—and we'll even point you in the direction of a 21st-century **Philly cheesesteak** along the way.

Franklin Court
316 Market Street

The most celebrated Philadelphian of all time is **Benjamin Franklin,** whose influence is seen throughout Philadelphia. The best place to learn about his life and accomplishments is within the cozy confines of Franklin Court. Look for the archway at 316 Market St. that leads to a clever "re-creation" of Franklin's house alongside a museum devoted to him.

Benjamin Franklin excelled in so many endeavors that it's hard to keep track of his achievements in the fields of science, diplomacy, business, education, publishing, and more. He may be the most accomplished man that America has ever produced.

Despite his renown, in 1812 his heirs razed his home to develop the site into more profitable uses. As the nation prepared for the

A clever "re-creation" of Franklin's house.

> **Burning Down the House**
>
> Franklin was living in London when the Stamp Act was passed by Parliament in 1765. The colonists believed the Stamp Act was an egregious example of "taxation without representation," yet Franklin was unaware of the outrage it created back home. He assigned a friend of his in Philadelphia, John Hughes, to collect the dreaded tax. This action was viewed by some in Philly as evidence that Franklin had "gone native" and now supported the king. A mob gathered outside Franklin's new home to burn it down. His wife Deborah grabbed a pistol and barricaded herself inside until a group of Franklin's supporters arrived and turned back the unruly gathering.

Bicentennial in 1976 there was interest in re-creating Franklin's house on its original site. Even though Franklin was one of the most famous men in America, there were no drawings of what his house looked like. Without such records how do you rebuild it? It turns out you don't. World-renowned Philadelphia architects Robert Venturi and Denise Scott Brown developed the minimalist form that became known as the **"Ghost House"**: a steel stick-figure of a building that was a clever way to portray the outline of the house and Franklin's printing office without resorting to a faux colonial-style structure.

Concrete portals allow a view down into the excavations that reveal the home's foundation. Since Franklin lived in London while the house was being built, he sent construction guidance via letters to his wife, Deborah. Some of his instructions are etched into the stone pavers surrounding the house.

Franklin Court is a tucked-away enclave for kids to run around and absorb some history in the process. Scattered throughout are stone circles embedded in the ground marking the privy pits and water wells of Franklin and his neighbors. Turn it into a scavenger hunt to see if the kids can find the one indicating "Franklin's Privy Pit 1787."

One of the first things visitors wonder is, what's the house doing tucked away back here? Shouldn't it be facing the street? Not according to the ever-thrifty Franklin, who left the valuable Market Street frontage for commercial buildings so he could collect higher rents from business tenants. Those buildings, which flank the arched entrance to Franklin Court on Market Street, now house the **B. Free Franklin Post Office** at 316 Market St. (it's an official United States Post Office) and a colonial-era printing office.

The unusual name for the post office stems from Franklin's term as postmaster general of the American colonies. One of the perks of the job was free postage, so he signed the envelopes "B. Free Franklin."

London Calling

If you want to step inside the only surviving house that Benjamin Franklin lived in, you need to head across the pond to London. He moved to the British capital in 1757 to represent the interests of the American colonies before the British Parliament and, aside from one return visit to America, he stayed in London until 1775. After a careful restoration, Franklin's London residence was opened to the public in 2006, coinciding with the 300th anniversary of his birth.

Franklin rented one room in the circa-1730 house at 36 Craven St., which backs up to Charing Cross Station. Most of the woodwork, windows, and floors in the house are original from Franklin's time. Visitors even ascend the same central staircase that Franklin climbed up and down as part of his daily exercise routine. **Prime Minister William Pitt** met regularly with Franklin in the small living room for consultations about the eroding relationship with America, effectively making the home the first American embassy in London.

Despite all the diplomatic intrigue, Franklin still devoted time to his inventions and developed the lightning rod in London. An original of his is still perched atop St. Paul's Cathedral.

The post office looks like a relic from the colonial era, but you can still mail letters and purchase stamps there. They'll even hand stamp your postcards with a postmark in Franklin's handwriting stating "B. Free Franklin." (*Note to kids:* Postcards are what your parents and grandparents sent to friends and family back home to brag that they were on vacation. It was a precursor to texting and Facebook and whatever newfangled tech app will be invented by the time you read this.)

But why is it the only post office in the United States that doesn't fly an American flag? Because when Franklin was a postmaster in pre-Revolutionary Philadelphia, the American flag hadn't been created yet. The post office is open 9 a.m. to 5 p.m. Mon through Sat and Franklin Court from 9 a.m. to dusk.

Franklin Court Printing Office
320 Market Street

One of 17 siblings and half-siblings, Benjamin Franklin initially trained to be a printer, apprenticing to his brother James in Boston. Due to his brother's mistreatment of him he ran away at age 17, first to New York and then on to Philadelphia to find a job. He arrived in October 1723; the very first day in town he spied a young woman named Deborah Read who would one day become his common-law wife.

He got a job at a printing shop and within a year met Governor William Keith who sent him to London to pick up supplies to start his own printing shop. Keith's connections didn't pan out, but Franklin stayed in London for a year and a half, honing his printing skills. Returning to Philadelphia he set up his own printing shop, which, through his diligence and cleverness, became a raging success. He stepped away from his business ventures when he was 42 and settled into a "retirement" life of scientific pursuits, education, politics, and diplomacy.

In the Printing Office adjacent to Franklin Court, National Park Rangers demonstrate 18th-century printing techniques and sell copies

The First Daughter of the American Revolution?
While Benjamin Franklin was handling American diplomatic matters in Europe, his daughter **Sarah Franklin Bache** kept the home fires burning. Or perhaps it would be better to say she helped keep the colonial army fired up.

Known as "Sally," Bache was an early member of the **Ladies' Association of Philadelphia,** a group of women founded in 1780 who raised money from local citizens to help support the colonial troops. Sally was a tireless fund-raiser, and stepped into the role of leader after the group's founder, **Esther Deberdt Reed,** died unexpectedly of dysentery. Franklin's daughter oversaw the acquisition of linens and the sewing of over 2,200 shirts to clothe the bedraggled colonial soldiers.

French delegates visiting Philadelphia during the war noticed Sally's efforts. François de Marbois, secretary to the minister from France, sent a letter to Benjamin Franklin in Paris in 1781, which commends his daughter: "If there are in Europe any women who need a model of attachment to domestic duties and love for their country, Mrs. Bache may be pointed out to them. She passed a part of the last year in exertions to rouse the zeal of the Pennsylvania ladies, and . . . a large part of the American army was provided with shirts, bought with their money, or made by their hands. She showed the most indefatigable zeal, [and] the most unwearied perseverance."

Sally Franklin stayed active in political circles after the war, acting as her widowed father's hostess until his death in 1790.

of documents they've made, including broadsides of the Declaration of Independence. Off to the side of the Printing Office is the restored office of Franklin's grandson, Benjamin Franklin Bache. He published a newspaper called the *Aurora;* just like his grandfather he spoke his mind when he argued against abuses of government power and was arrested in 1798 for libeling President John Adams.

In paintings and sculpture Franklin is usually depicted as a chubby old man. But in his early years he must have been in great shape. As the

Better than working out at the gym: Try yanking on this 4,000 times a day.

Park Rangers demonstrate, printing was a physically demanding job. Various job titles such as "puller" and "beater" hint at the hard work involved. When the paper was slid onto the type, the printer vigorously pulled the long wooden handle on the press so the type forced the ink onto the paper hard enough to leave a mark. This was done twice for each sheet of paper, and a typical printer cranked out 2,000 sheets per day—that's 4,000 yanks on the press.

The rangers also demonstrate some of the difficulties in reading colonial-era manuscripts, since some of the letters looked different back then. They had a long "s" that looked like a present-day "f" so when it appeared in a word other than at the end it looks to modern readers like an "f." Here's a phrase published by Franklin in *Poor Richard's Almanack* in 1736. To modern eyes it looks like, "Fifh and vifitors ftink after three days." But what the acerbic Franklin was saying was, "Fish and

Mind Your P's and Q's

Several common phrases come from the world of printing. When a printer laid out the type they were handling tiny pieces of metal with the letters forged backwards so they showed up correctly when printed on the page. The lowercase "p" and "q" are mirror images of each other, so apprentices were admonished to be aware of those letters. The concept of upper- and lowercase letters come from printing too. We know uppercase letters as capital letters and lowercase letters as small letters. But how did they get those names? The printer's type was stored in wooden cases by the press. The capital letters were stored in the upper case and the small letters were stored in, you guessed it, the lower case. It's as simple as that.

visitors stink after three days." Keep that in mind when you're unfurling an old parchment to peruse. Otherwise you may end up sounding like Elmer Fudd.

Franklin Court Printing Office Information

Location: 320 Market St.

Hours: Open daily 10 a.m. to 5 p.m.

Admission: Free

Phone: (215) 965-2305

Website: nps.gov/inde/planyourvisit/franklin-court-printing-office.htm

Wheelchair accessibility: The Printing Office is wheelchair accessible.

Ben There, Done That:

A Timeline of Benjamin Franklin's Life

1706: Born in Boston

1715: Develops his first invention, wooden paddles for swimming

1723: While apprenticing as a printer to an older brother he runs away to Philadelphia

1725: Moves to London and works in a printing office

1726: Returns to Philadelphia

1727: Founds the Leather Apron Club, known as the Junto. This social group of 12 men becomes the springboard for many of Franklin's inventions and ideas. Members were craftsmen like Franklin who wore leather aprons to work.

1728: Opens printing office

1730: Enters common-law marriage with Deborah Read

1731: Starts the Library Company of Philadelphia, the nation's first successful lending library

1733: First publishes *Poor Richard's Almanack*, a perennial bestseller

1736: Founds Philadelphia's first organized firefighting unit

1743: Founds the American Philosophical Society to promote "useful knowledge" in the sciences and humanities

1749: Founds the school that would become the University of Pennsylvania

1751: Along with Dr. Thomas Bond, cofounds Pennsylvania Hospital, the first hospital in America

1751: Publishes *Experiments and Observations on Electricity: Made in Philadelphia and America*. It's considered the most significant scientific work to come out of the American colonies and the first practical guide to electricity

1752: Per longstanding legend, performs his electrical experiments with a kite and a key in a lightning storm

1752: Cofounds first fire insurance company

1753: First nonnative of Great Britain to win the prestigious Copley Medal, awarded by the Royal Society of London for scientific achievement

1757 to 1762: Lives in London as colonial agent to Great Britain

1762: First American to invent a musical instrument, the glass
armonica
1764: Sails back to London where he lives until he returns to
Philadelphia in 1775
1774: Wife Deborah dies while Franklin is in London
1775: Appointed first postmaster general by Congress
1776: Signs the Declaration of Independence
1776 to 1785: Lives in Paris to create an alliance supporting the
colonies
1783: Signs the Treaty of Paris, which ended the American
Revolution
1784: Invents bifocal glasses
1787: Signs the US Constitution
1790: Dies at the age of 84; funeral attended by 20,000 mourn-
ers, about two-thirds the population of Philadelphia
1914: First appears on the $100 bill

Benjamin Franklin Museum
318 Market Street (through the archway)

After a two-year closure during which it was completely overhauled, the Benjamin Franklin Museum reopened in August 2013, replacing a Bicentennial-era facility that was showing its age. The new museum is of the "please touch" variety, so it's a nifty place to bring children to roam and play with the interactive exhibits and touch-screen displays. They might even learn a thing or two about Philadelphia's favorite son in the process. The entrance is by the "Ghost House" replica of Franklin's home.

Upon entering the museum you'll be confronted with one of the paradoxes of Franklin's life: Even though he was an abolitionist in his later years, he owned slaves until he was in his 60s, freeing them a few years before the Revolution. One display reveals that when Franklin and his son William moved to London in 1757, they brought along two slaves, King and Peter; King promptly escaped. Visitors are left to form their own opinions about how Franklin fit into the social mores of his era.

The museum showcases Franklin's many inventions and scientific pursuits. Franklin invented an instrument called a **glass armonica,** a device that produces musical notes by rubbing a series of horizontally spinning glass bowls. In the process Franklin became the first American to invent a musical instrument. Deborah Franklin called the sound "the music of angels." An armonica from 1761 that Franklin owned is on display next to a game that could be called "Glass Armonica Hero." Try your hand at playing "Yankee Doodle Dandy" by tapping the touch-screen, which shows a spinning armonica with

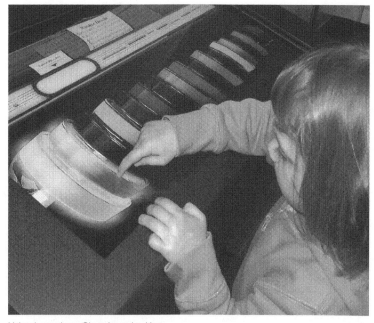

Unleash your inner Glass Armonica Hero.

color-coded bowls matching a series of notes. Nearby, Sudoku fans can play Magic Squares, a numerical game Franklin invented to keep himself amused.

Franklin or bust at the gift shop.

> **Talking Turkey**
>
> Franklin developed a method to generate and store electrical impulses; a walnut-and-iron box filled with glass Leyden jars that he used for this purpose is on display at the museum. It's really a giant battery—Franklin was the first to apply to that term to the field of electricity. At Christmastime in 1750 Franklin got the big fat idea that if he shocked his holiday turkey it would tenderize the meat, so he set up an experiment to try it. After all, what could go wrong? Apparently, a lot. Instead of tenderizing the turkey, the bespectacled inventor violently shocked himself instead, feeling "a powerful surge from head to foot." He was sore for a few days after and embarrassed for longer than that. There's no record of how the turkey tasted.

Budding scientists will enjoy, or perhaps be grossed out, peering through a microscope for a close-up view of butterfly wings, a peacock feather, or human skin (ick!). Interactive quizzes with questions related to Franklin's life respond with hearty cries of "huzzah" when you guess the correct answer. An animated cartoon shows Franklin splashing in a stream as he demonstrates a rudimentary form of kite sailing he invented. Franklin's first invention was at the age of 14 when

> **Benjamin Franklin Museum Information**
>
> **Location:** 318 Market St. Enter through either the arched courtyard at 318 Market St. or the alley next to 321 Chestnut St.
>
> **Hours:** Open daily 9 a.m. to 5 p.m.
>
> **Admission:** Adults, $5; children, $2; ages 3 and under, free.
>
> **Phone:** (215) 965-2305
>
> **Website:** nps.gov/inde/planyourvisit/benjaminfranklinmuseum.htm
>
> **Wheelchair accessibility:** Fully accessible

he developed wooden swim flippers that, much like an artist's palette, attached to the swimmer's hands. In fact, he's the only Founding Father in the **International Swimming Hall of Fame.**

Pit Stop: Sonny's Famous Cheesesteaks & Burgers

No trip to Philadelphia would be complete without sampling one of the city's eponymous **cheesesteaks.** Thinly sliced beef grilled with

---

Cheesesteak Etiquette

The Philly cheesesteak is no longer just a local delicacy; the sandwich pops up on menus all over the globe. Here are a few things to know when ordering the real deal in Philadelphia:

- It is always a "cheesesteak," never a "Philly steak" (or heaven forbid a "steak and cheese"). For the lactose-intolerant, you get one without cheese and call it a "steak sandwich" or simply a "steak."

- Purists ask for either American or Provolone cheese, depending on your preference. We personally like American; it melts better.

- What about Cheez Whiz? Now there's an argument-starter. Some swear by it, while other shops won't even carry it, saying it's not real cheese. If you do decide to go the processed-food route, order "Whiz," never "Cheez Whiz."

- If you want grilled onions (recommended), you order your steak "with," or in the local lingo, "wit."

- Grilled peppers are not typical. Philadelphians might garnish their cheesesteaks with hot or sweet peppers, but they will usually be the pickled variety.

- The condiment of choice is ketchup. Not mayo, not mustard, not tomato sauce.

    Now that you're up on all the etiquette, go up to the counter, order your "cheesesteak, American, with," top it with ketchup, and prepare for a true taste of Philadelphia.

---

caramelized onions and mixed with melting cheese all nestled into a long roll is a culinary joy to savor—if it's done right.

Using only fresh thinly sliced ribeye for the steaks and 100 percent Angus beef for the burgers, the sandwiches here are a cut above standard walk-up window fare found elsewhere in the city. For a gourmet touch Sonny's also offers a choice of some fancy toppings, such as blue cheese and applewood-smoked bacon. Non-meat-eaters can order grilled cheese, which Sonny's offers on thick-sliced brioche bread.

Cheesesteaks are not small sandwiches; the roll is about a foot long, so unless you're super hungry you may want to share. Sonny's has a few tables inside, and outdoor seating is available on the large sidewalk out front in warmer weather.

Sonny's Famous Cheesesteaks and Burgers is located at 238 Market St. and is open 11 a.m. to 10 p.m. Sun to Thurs, 11 a.m. to 3 a.m. (yes, that's 3 *a.m.* for you night owls) Fri and Sat.

Christ Church
20 North American Street (near North 2nd Street just north of Market Street)

With a roster of worshippers that included George Washington, Benjamin Franklin, and several signers of the Declaration of Independence, Christ Church is often referred to as the "Nation's Church." George Thomas in *Buildings of Pennsylvania: Philadelphia and Eastern Pennsylvania* calls it "as perfect and historic a church as there is in the United States."

Looking at Christ Church today, in its understated bucolic setting off the main thoroughfare of Market Street, it's hard to imagine the sheer audacity it took to build this refined structure. When the Anglicans started construction in 1727 to replace their original 1696 wood frame church, Philadelphia was a small, predominantly Quaker country town with pigs roaming unpaved muddy streets.

Christ Church is one of the most elegant colonial buildings.

By building the large elegant church less than half a century after Quaker William Penn founded Philadelphia, the Anglicans were making their mark on the growing city. Some Anglicans viewed their Quaker neighbors as misled and perhaps even a bit subversive. Remember, one of the reasons Quakers were persecuted in England was that they refused to take an oath of loyalty to the Crown. There was no such problem with Anglicans, who had royalty in their corner by claiming the reigning British monarch as the head of their church.

Christ Church may be the most spectacular remaining example of early American architecture. According to church historian Neil Ronk, its construction reveals "the cockiness of 18th-century Philadelphia. The city wanted to be the London of America." What better way to do this than to dream up a church whose design seemed purloined from the plans of London's top architects?

Despite all this bravado, the new church building wasn't finished until 1744, and it took another 10 years to raise sufficient cash for the steeple. A few of the names on the subscription list for the steeple and a set of bells are seen elsewhere on the Philadelphia Liberty Trail and reveal how close-knit the upper echelons of society were in colonial Philadelphia: there was **Benjamin Franklin,** of course, along with his son **William Franklin; Philip Syng,** the silversmith who crafted the inkwell used to sign the Declaration of Independence; and **Charles Stedman,** the builder of the Powel House.

Robert Smith, the architect of **Carpenters' Hall** and **St. Peter's Church,** designed the steeple. In an impressive display of colonial-era engineering, it soared 200 feet from the base to the top of the lightning rod, making Christ Church the tallest building in America (beating Old North Church in Boston by 3 feet), a title it held until 1810. The church's commanding height was symbolic of the growing Anglican influence in Philadelphia; within five years the Quakers were no longer in the majority.

Reverend William White became rector in 1778, a position he held until his death in 1836. After the war White sailed to Great Britain to be ordained as first bishop of the Protestant Episcopal Church in America, and later helped create the **Episcopal Church** in America when it broke away from the Anglican Communion. Bishop White's

---

Penn's Payback

Christ Church was the tallest building in America for 56 years, until it was displaced by Boston's Park Street Church in 1810. In 1901 William Penn snagged the title back when an immense statue in his likeness topped Philadelphia's City Hall, making it not only the tallest building in America, but in the entire world. "Billy" Penn stayed on top for seven years, until the Singer Building in New York eclipsed him in 1908.

At Christ Church, a recent immigrant from London would have felt right at home.

house is now part of Independence Park and is a stop on the Philadelphia Liberty Trail.

The church's sanctuary, with its varying shades of cream, ecru, and white lit by the sun's rays through the clear glass windows, seems like heaven on Earth. The first impression is of the grand unadorned Palladian window anchoring the eastern wall behind the altar along with the soaring fluted columns supporting the arched ceiling trusses. The interior represents the height of sophistication and was a shining example of the technical and artistic achievements of the "country bumpkins" in colonial America.

The wine-glass pulpit hovers over the burial marker for John Penn, who was the governor of Pennsylvania until 1776 and a grandson of William. Note pew #70 where Benjamin Franklin sat, although his attendance wasn't as regular as his wife and daughter's. Franklin's calling took a more practical form: He was active in helping with church

Baptism by Fire

Don't miss the wooden baptismal font, which is over 400 years old. It was brought over in 1697 from the church of All Hallows by the Tower in London, a congregation that was founded in 675 AD. (That's not a typo. You think things are old in Philadelphia; in London they are positively ancient.) It's the same font in which the infant **William Penn** was baptized in London, as were Benjamin Franklin's children in Philadelphia, and it's still used for baptisms today.

William Penn's father, **Admiral Sir William Penn,** is credited with saving All Hallows during the **Great Fire of London** in 1666, an event that would ultimately impact the layout of Philadelphia. He ordered men from the nearby docks to tear down structures around the church to create firebreaks. Afterwards, he and his neighbor, noted diarist Samuel Pepys, climbed the tower and watched the inferno engulf London. The Great Fire of London had a strong influence on William Penn's rectilinear site plan for the city of Philadelphia, which was designed with space between buildings to avoid massive fires that could wipe out the city.

Penn's baptismal font.

fund-raising efforts when needed. The resourceful Franklin was drawn to the church as the place where up-and-coming entrepreneurs went to "see and be seen."

The walk through history continues with a choice selection of Christ Church's artifacts. The silver communion set donated by Queen Anne in 1708 is brought out for feast days. High-end Philadelphia cabinetmaker John Folwell crafted the pulpit; he also fashioned the famous "Rising Sun" chair in Independence Hall.

There is a small burial ground in the churchyard adjacent to the building that includes prominent early Americans, including two signers of the Declaration of Independence, **Robert Morris,** who helped finance the Revolution, along with **James Wilson;** the **Reverend William White;** and **Andrew Hamilton,** one of the designers of Independence Hall.

The growth of the congregation required the purchase of land in 1719 a few blocks away at 5th and Arch Streets for a larger burial ground. That's another stop on the Philadelphia Liberty Trail and also

---

Bells, Books, and Candles

The bell for the original church came from Whitechapel Foundry in London (the casters of the precursor to the Liberty Bell) in 1702 and is the oldest church bell in Pennsylvania. It's now on display in the sanctuary, where it was recently rung at the request of a blind child who was filled with glee to hear a bell that Thomas Jefferson also heard—what a stirring way to experience history.

Among the church's artifacts are many rare books including an 18th-century **Book of Common Prayer,** which by order of the Vestry on July 4, 1776, was edited by Reverend Jacob Duché to omit prayers for the king and the royal family.

The original candlelit chandelier that still hangs in the sanctuary was imported from London. It cast its glow on the wedding of **Sarah Franklin,** Benjamin's daughter, in 1767.

---

the final resting place for Benjamin Franklin. The ever-thrifty Franklin didn't even have to buy his own burial plot; his wife Deborah's family were members of Christ Church and already owned one.

Christ Church Information

Address: 20 N. American St. (near North 2nd Street just north of Market Street)

Hours: The church is open 9 a.m. to 5 p.m. Mon through Sat, 1 p.m. to 5 p.m. Sun. Services on Sun at 9 a.m. and 11 a.m. Closed Mon and Tues in Jan and Feb, New Year's Day, Easter Sunday, Thanksgiving, and Christmas.

Admission: Free, with a suggested donation of $3 for adults and $2 for students.

Phone: (215) 922-1695

Website: christchurchphila.org

Wheelchair accessibility: Through 2nd Street entrance

Pit Stop: The Franklin Fountain and Shane Confectionery

All this historical immersion will no doubt put you in the mood for some "retro" refreshment, for which there's no better spot than **The Franklin Fountain.** Step into this old-time corner ice-cream parlor and soda fountain for some tasty treats. The owners, brothers Ryan and Eric Berley, are passionate about authenticity and have faithfully re-created an early 1900s soda fountain, both in decor and ingredients; even the "soda jerks" are dressed in period attire.

All of the ice creams are handmade in-house, sporting top-notch flavorings such as real fruit purees, maple syrup, and whole roasted nuts. Sundaes are an event—creative concoctions with homemade sauces and freshly whipped cream on top. Try a Stock Market Crunch: Rocky

Road ice cream coated in peanut butter sauce and crumbled pretzels. The mammoth portions are big enough to share—a good thing because these high-quality ingredients don't come cheap.

No soda fountain would be complete without a selection of fizzy drinks; the Franklin Fountain offers a wide selection of "phosphates," malts, and other goodies, all made to order. Summer is the perfect season for a refreshing lime rickey with freshly pressed limes; in winter you might want to try hot cocoa or a "hot milkshake."

The Franklin Fountain is popular, so in summer lines can be long. If you're fortunate enough to snag one of the few tables, your concoction will come in a nifty old-time glass dish.

Just down the block, **Shane Confectionery** has been in the sweets business since 1911. It's now owned by the Franklin Fountain's Berley brothers, who oversee the traditional hand-rolling of chocolate buttercreams and pouring of hard candies into antique molds.

Pop in and browse the marble counter for a box of the famous hand-rolled chocolates, or perhaps pick up some of the vintage candy brands on display.

The Franklin Fountain is located 116 Market St. and is open seven days a week noon to midnight, cash only.

Shane Confectionery is located at 110 Market St. and is open Mon through Thurs noon to 7 p.m., Fri and Sat 11 a.m. to 10 p.m., and Sun 11 a.m. to 7 p.m.

Elfreth's Alley

Elfreth's Alley and North Second Street (1.5 blocks north of Market Street)

Billed as the "oldest continually occupied street in America," Elfreth's Alley is a delightful grouping of 32 homes, tucked snugly around a block-long cobblestoned street. With its well-maintained compact brick

It's always the 18th century on Elfreth's Alley.

houses, the earliest of which date to the 1720s, framed by colorful wooden shutters, it looks like something out of a Hollywood back lot for a colonial-era film shoot. The street presents a remarkable opportunity to get a sense of what daily life was like in pre-Revolutionary Philadelphia. Well, minus the early 18th-century smells and sounds. At least today you don't have to watch where you step.

To really understand Elfreth's Alley it helps to learn a bit about town planning in Philadelphia. We've talked elsewhere about Penn's original plan for a "greene Country Towne" that was radical in its design. The streets were laid out at right angles, and the houses were to be placed in the middle of their lots, surrounded by gardens. It all sounds so quaint.

The reality turned out to be much different, creating what came to be the most congested town in America. The streets are still laid out at right angles, but what happened to the grand houses that were supposed to be set amidst plush greenery?

Philadelphia from its inception was one giant real-estate play, a sort of colonial-era Monopoly game with William Penn as the landlord. He meant well, but his vision for the city soon met up with market forces. Just as you win in Monopoly by putting more houses on the same patch of ground, the early settlers figured out how to make their lots more valuable.

The lots Penn and his surveyor Thomas Holme laid out were too long and narrow to be efficient, so the owners subdivided them into smaller lots. Then those lots needed access for the new owners to get to them, so connecting streets and alleys were built. Philadelphia is riddled with these pocket-sized alleys called **cartways,** some only 6 feet wide, that were used by workmen hauling goods. Though they are quaint

Can you tell these two houses were built by brothers?

> **Court Proceedings**
> Tucked within the narrow confines of Elfreth's Alley is a hidden gem called **Bladen's Court**. One of the residents who lived there was a carpenter named **Abraham Carlisle,** who was accused of aiding the redcoats during the British occupation of Philadelphia in 1777–78. After the British skipped town Carlisle was tried for treason and, in a controversial decision, hanged on the town square.

streets to live on today, they went against Penn's plan to keep houses far enough apart to prevent major fires sweeping through the city.

Elfreth's Alley was created in 1702 by blacksmiths John Gilbert and Arthur Wells, to connect their shops with the Delaware River waterfront. They each gave up a bit of their land to carve out the new passageway. Looking towards the Delaware River now, with the Berlin Wall-like edifice of I-95 blocking the way both visually and physically, it's easy to forget that Philadelphia was a town that survived and thrived based on its river access. The alley became an easy shortcut for Gilbert, Wells, and others greeting incoming ships and offloading provisions. Naturally the next step in development was to build houses along the new street, which started thrumming with artisans, traders, and newly arrived immigrants seeking shelter.

Built between 1724 and 1728, the twin houses at 120 and 122 are the two oldest on the street. After a few years owners Andrew Edge

> **What's in a Name?**
> The Philadelphia region is known as the **Delaware Valley,** but it's not named after the Delaware tribe of Native Americans. Rather, they, and the Delaware River and the state of Delaware, were named after Sir Thomas West, the 12th Baron De La Warr and governor of the English colony at Jamestown, Virginia, in 1610.

and Thomas Potts discovered that they had each mistakenly built their homes on the other's lot. They must have gotten along; the homes are connected internally via a "gossip door."

Notice how some of the homes have a skinny metal contraption sticking out of the second-floor window like a giant spider leg? It's called a "busybody" and is used by the homeowner to peer below and see who's knocking at the door. What a bit of colonial ingenuity to ward off door-to-door salesmen!

Elfreth's Alley Information

Location: Elfreth's Alley is a public street located on the east side of North 2nd Street 1.5 blocks north of Market Street. The Elfreth's Alley Museum is at 124–126 Elfreth's Alley.

Hours: The street is open 24/7. Summer hours for the Elfreth's Alley Museum are generally 12 to 5 p.m. Fri, Sat, and Sun. Museum and alley tours are usually offered at noon and 3 p.m. The rest of the year is subject to change. *Note:* These hours are variable. It's always best to check ahead of time.

Special Events: First Saturday in June is Fete Day when some of the houses are open to the public. First Saturday in December is "Deck the Alley," when houses are decorated for Christmas and open to the public. Check the calendar at elfreths .blogspot.com/p/events-calendar for these and other events.

Admission: As a public street Elfreth's Alley is free. Museum admission: adults, $5; children 6 to 12 years old, $2; $12 per family; free for children under 6. Guided tours of the alley are also offered. Call ahead to find out the schedule.

Phone: (215) 627-8680

Website: elfrethsalley.org

Wheelchair accessibility: The street is accessible but is rough cobblestone.

Note: Be aware that although Elfreth's Alley is a public street, the homes on it are private residences.

▣ Fighting Fire with . . . Insurance

For a fun scavenger hunt in Philadelphia gaze up at the façades of old brick buildings throughout the historic district. Many of them display football-sized lead plaques shaped like ovals, rectangles, and shields. The emblems on them vary; the more common ones are a leafy tree, four hands, and an eagle. These are called "fire marks."

Fire marks served multiple purposes: Painted with the owner's policy number, they signified that the homeowner carried fire insurance and were helpful in identifying houses in the event of a fire. They were also an early form of advertising for the insurance company. Even more so than today, fire was the dreaded scourge of cities in times past. The Great Fire of London that

A typical fire mark.

wiped out most of the town in 1666 was very much on William Penn's mind when he laid out Philadelphia in a grid pattern.

The oldest marks are those with four intertwined hands. In 1752 the Philadelphia Contributionship, a property insurance company founded by Benjamin Franklin and still located in its circa-1835 headquarters at 212 S. 4th St., attached them to their customers' houses.

The Mutual Assurance Company, founded in 1784, issued fire marks with a tree. At the time trees were considered hazardous to a property, so companies wouldn't insure houses with trees. The Mutual Assurance Company was apparently "green" two centuries before that notion became popular and placed a tree on their fire mark to indicate they had no issues with the "dreaded" foliage.

To view a wide selection of fire marks, along with a collection of antique firefighting equipment, head over to the Fireman's Hall Museum at 147 N. 2nd St., a half-block north of Elfreth's Alley.

Elfreth's Alley isn't just about a quaintly preserved cobblestoned street highlighting colonial architecture. It also celebrates the ordinary working people who lived here, in a way that isn't viewed when touring opulent mansions. In 1934 resident **Dorothy Ottey** spearheaded the effort to save Elfreth's Alley, preserving it so visitors can experience a remnant of authentic colonial life.

The **Elfreth's Alley Museum** is at 124–126 Elfreth's Alley in two rowhomes built by Jeremiah Elfreth in 1762. They convey a sense of residential life on the street for the past 300 years. The museum is restored and furnished as it was in 1790 when two female dressmakers occupied it. Exhibits reveal the lifestyle of blue-collar workers in early America, including the changes that the rise of the Industrial Revolution brought to this compact neighborhood.

Side Trip: Fireman's Hall Museum

A few steps north of Elfreth's Alley is a restored 1902 firehouse that is the home of the Fireman's Hall Museum. Operated by the Fire Prevention Unit of the Philadelphia Fire Department and staffed by active firefighters, the museum has a dual role: to present the colorful history of firefighting in one of America's oldest fire departments and to promote fire-prevention awareness.

Artifacts include leather buckets, cast-iron fire marks that were placed on buildings as proof of fire insurance, a wall of axes, and old firefighting rigs including a horse-drawn fire engine from 1858 that is the oldest steam engine in America. When the volunteer firefighters from Philadelphia Hose Company #1 commissioned the apparatus from Reaney & Neafie shipbuilders the steam technology was still experimental, but it worked. Suddenly a job that took fifty men on a hand-pumped engine could be performed by three, and firefighting was never the same.

Kids will enjoy trying on actual firefighting turnout gear and swaying under the weight of the equipment. The museum also offers a scavenger hunt for younger children; ask the firefighter at the front desk about it.

Just be aware that even though there is a brass pole in the corner that firemen used to slide down from the second floor as they raced to a fire, visitors are not allowed to copy them. Believe us, we asked.

The Fireman's Hall Museum is located at 147 N. 2nd St. Hours are 10 a.m. to 4:30 p.m. Tues through Sat, open until 9 p.m. the first Fri of the month when Old City art galleries are open late. Call (215) 923-1438 or check online at firemanshall.org for further information.

Pit Stop: Tartes Fine Cakes and Pastries

Sometimes a cookie is just the ticket for taking the edge off a busy day of historic exploration. The smell of butter-infused goodies wafting out of the ovens at Tartes will have grumpy travelers smiling again in no time. This petite (dare we say tart-sized?) bakery offers up a rotating selection of single-serving delicacies from a walk-up window. Award-winning chocolate chip cookies, red velvet cupcakes, and chewy brownies are just a few of the hand-held treats to try. You might even want to bring a few of the namesake "tartes" back to your hotel for later.

Tartes Fine Cakes and Pastries is located at 212 Arch St. and is open 10 a.m. to 7 p.m. Tues to Sat.

Betsy Ross House
239 Arch Street

Early in the summer of 1776 George Washington, Robert Morris, and George Ross went to the Arch Street upholstery shop of a young widow named Elizabeth Griscom

The Betsy Ross House is a colonial survivor on Arch Street.

Ross and asked her to make a flag for the new country. She showed them how to make stars with five points instead of six . . .

So goes the legend of **Betsy Ross.** This was the tale told by her grandchildren in the 1870s, a story that many historians doubt. But before we get too embroiled in this "legendary" debate, let's explore what is known about this remarkable woman who was a patriot, a successful entrepreneur, and a single working mom.

Although Elizabeth "Betsy" Griscom was born into a Quaker family, her temperament seemed suited to the cause of liberty. In November of 1773, at the age of 21, she eloped with John Ross, a fellow upholstery apprentice at the shop where she worked. Her new beau was not a Quaker, so she braved being disowned and "read out" of the Quaker faith.

The young couple set up their own upholstery shop on Chestnut Street. John Ross died in early 1776, so after only two years of marriage Betsy Ross found herself widowed at the age of 23, with a business to run in a country on the brink of war.

An upholsterer in 18th-century Philadelphia spent his or her time crafting bed hangings, chair cushions, and window treatments for the elegant homes that were popping up in the growing city. Impending war might curtail demand for such domestic extravagances, but it would offer a new business opportunity for upholsterers in the making of tents, mattresses—and flags.

In the 18th century, flags served a practical function. With their bright colors and geometric designs waving in the breeze, they were a means of identification for troops on the battlefield or for sailors at sea.

For a young widow struggling to keep her business afloat, sewing flags for the new Continental Army provided much-needed work, and it's known that Betsy made American flags. But did she sew the first? Here's where historical facts mingle with family lore. In 1870 Betsy's grandson William Canby and more of her descendants released

A star is born.

sworn affidavits stating they heard their grandmother/mother/aunt relate the story of how she made the first flag at the request of George Washington.

Canby asserted that Washington came to the shop along with Robert Morris and George Ross and presented Betsy with a design of a flag with 13 red and white stripes and 13 six-pointed stars on a field of blue. Betsy suggested changing the stars to a five-pointed design, showing the gentlemen how it would be quicker to produce by folding the fabric a certain way and making a single cut.

There are no records or receipts relating to the production of this first "Betsy Ross" flag, creating the debate with historians. But these were chaotic times. During his two-week visit to Philadelphia in the spring of 1776, General Washington was a busy man. The Continental Congress had just authorized $50,000 for the commander-in-chief to acquire "sundry articles for the use of the continental army," which included flags, or "colours." Washington needed the services of many tradesmen (and women) who could assist with this task.

Since her late husband's uncle, George Ross, was active in government oversight of the military, Betsy Ross would likely have been contacted. Other potential suppliers of sewn goods for the fledgling military—including Cornelia Bridges, Margaret Manny, and Rebecca Flower Young—were probably approached as well. By the spring of 1777, recordkeeping was more consistent and documentation firmly establishes Betsy Ross as a flag maker for the revolutionary government.

In mid 1777 Betsy married Joseph Ashburn. Over the next few years she gave birth to two daughters; one died as an infant. Her new husband was a mariner who spent much of his time at sea, often leaving Betsy to manage her shop (now on Arch Street) and her young family alone during the turbulent Revolutionary War years. In 1781, when their daughter Eliza was just six months old, Joseph Ashburn

---

Heavens to Betsy!

Surviving three marriages, Betsy Ross certainly availed herself of William Penn's Charter of Privileges granting religious freedom in the City of Brotherly Love. Born a Quaker, she attended **Bank Street Meeting House** (no longer standing) as a child. She was banished from the Quaker faith after her elopement with John Ross, so the couple attended the Anglican **Christ Church.** She married her second husband John Ashburn at then Lutheran **Old Swede's Church** (found in the Farther Afield section of this book). Betsy returned to **Christ Church** for the marriage to her third husband, John Claypoole. Shortly after her marriage to Claypoole, Betsy returned to her Quaker roots—sort of. She and John joined the **Free (or "Fighting") Quaker Meeting House** (also on the Philadelphia Liberty Trail). Both John and Betsy were buried in the Free Quaker Burial Ground before their remains were ultimately moved to the Betsy Ross House courtyard.

again took to the waves. The British captured Ashburn's ship at sea and he was imprisoned in England, where he died in 1782. By the end of the war Betsy had become a widow twice, and now had a child to support.

Betsy continued to make flags for the US government well into her 70s, including dozens on the eve of the War of 1812; she even worked with her third husband, John Claypoole, in the trade after they married in 1783. They would ultimately raise an additional five children together. Elizabeth Griscom Ross Ashburn Claypoole died in 1836 at the age of 84, not yet the legendary figure she is today. Ironically, Betsy and John Ross had no children; the descendants who perpetuated her oral history were Ashburns and Claypooles.

So did Betsy make the first flag? We will likely never know for certain. But as historian Marla Miller states in her critically acclaimed biography *Betsy Ross and the Making of America*,

> *Much like . . . countless other contested "firsts" in American history the evidence reminds us that the did-she-or-didn't-she question is not especially useful. . . . Many people helped form the national emblem we recognize today. That Betsy Ross was not alone does not diminish her contribution among them. The flag, like the Revolution it represents, was the work of many hands.*

The Betsy Ross House on Arch Street is a circa-1760 brick house and shop faithfully restored to what it is believed to have looked like during the years surrounding the Revolutionary War. The small townhouse is typical of the shops and homes that stood on Arch Street 250 years ago (much like the homes on **Elfreth's Alley**). According to Ross's descendants, Betsy rented the front part of the building during those years for a shop on the main floor, with living quarters above.

Thy Spy

Betsy Ross's story passed down via oral tradition through her family, much like the tale of one of the unsung heroes of the American Revolution, **Lydia Darragh,** who was also a Quaker. Darragh was a native of Ireland living in Philadelphia when the British occupied the city. She stayed behind when her son Charles left to serve in the Continental Army. By chance she lived across the street from the tavern that the British high command had requisitioned for their headquarters. Occasionally they'd use a room in Darragh's house to hold late-night strategy sessions. During one of these, Darragh overheard the officers finalizing plans for a surprise attack on Washington's troops at their encampment in nearby Whitemarsh, where her son Charles was stationed. She set out from Philadelphia to alert the army, meeting up with an American officer to whom she passed along the information. When the attack came the Americans easily repelled it, sending the British army fleeing back to the comfort of Philadelphia. Darragh didn't go public with her tale, but relayed it to her children who passed it down through the generations of the family, although others questioned its veracity. But in 1905 the memoirs of the officer who received the warning that night were found and published, and he mentioned a woman handing the details to him outside the city limits. While it's impossible to know if Lydia Darragh was that person, it certainly gives credence to her story that she had a hand in foiling a disastrous attack on the American troops.

A self-guided tour takes visitors through rooms furnished as they were in the late 18th century, up and down wedge-shaped "butterfly steps" showing living quarters, the upholstery shop, and storeroom. A highlight of the tour is meeting "Betsy Ross," a historical re-enactor in the shop. "Betsy" never breaks character, answering questions in 18th-century vernacular, demonstrating to visitors how to craft a perfect five-pointed star from a folded piece of paper with a single cut.

![icon] Young children particularly enjoy the ground-floor storeroom and kitchen, where a "please touch" section includes toy food and utensils, along with recipes for 18th-century victuals.

The tour concludes in the shaded brick courtyard next to the house, where **Elizabeth Griscom Ross Ashburn Claypoole,** the nation's beloved Betsy Ross, is buried with her third husband John Claypoole.

Betsy Ross House Information

Location: 239 Arch St.

Hours: 10 a.m. to 5 p.m. daily, Mar through Nov; closed Mon, Dec through Feb.

Admission: Adults $5; children, students, seniors, and military $4. A self-guided audio tour is available for an additional $2. Admission to the courtyard and Betsy Ross's grave is free.

Phone: (215) 629-4026

Website: historicphiladelphia.org/betsy-ross-house/what-to-see

Wheelchair accessibility: The courtyard is accessible; the remainder of the house is not accessible.

Pit Stop: Humphrys Flag Company

If you owned a flag company, could you think of a better place for your shop than across the street from the Betsy Ross House? The location seems to work for the Humphrys Flag Company, which has been in Philadelphia since 1864.

According to Matt O'Connor, the "CFO" (that's "chief flag officer" to us regular folk), Humphrys is the only remaining company in the US that still manufactures all its flags in America. In 1996 they set a Guinness World Record when their immense custom-made American flag was unfurled from the top of Hoover Dam.

Another day at the office for the chief flag officer.

Humphrys is the place to acquire a flag of any state, country (they even have North Korea), or military branch, along with historic flags from America's colonial days. If visiting the Betsy Ross House has got you fired up with patriotic fervor to fly a 13-star American flag on your front stoop, Humphrys will have it. They also carry a large selection of flag-related hardware: poles, finials, and brackets for displaying the Stars and Stripes.

Humphrys Flag Company is located at 238 Arch St. and is open Mon to Fri 8 a.m. to 5 p.m., Sat 11 a.m. to 4 p.m., or by appointment, closed Sun; (215) 922-0510; humphrysflag.com.

Arch Street Friends Meeting House
320 Arch Street

The circa-1804 and 1811 Arch Street Friends Meeting House is the oldest meeting house still operating in Philadelphia. The simple lines and brickwork reflect austere Quaker principles, which shun ostentation and undue ornamentation in their lives. The Religious Society of Friends, more commonly known as Quakers, used the Arch Street site as a burial ground on land granted to them by William Penn, a function it served for over 100 years before the new meeting house was built.

The building's designer, the self-described "house carpenter and teacher of architectural drawing" **Owen Biddle,** was a Quaker himself. In 1805 he wrote *The Young Carpenter's Assistant; or a System of Architecture Adapted to the Style of Building in the United States.* It's considered the first architectural textbook in the United States and one of the most influential building-design books ever. Biddle died just a year later at age 32 and is buried on-site.

Quaker Oaths

During the American Revolution citizens were required to swear loyalty to the new regime. This was a problem for Quakers on several levels. Their faith prohibited them from swearing loyalty to any government. In addition, such an oath would be seen as supporting the violence that was taking place, going against their pacifist principles. Such steadfastness to their beliefs cost many of them dearly. Already under suspicion and harassed for refusing to join the military, in some instances they were seen as traitors and expelled from Philadelphia. On the eve of the British occupation of Philadelphia in September 1777, 17 Quaker men were banished to Virginia. Their experience contrasts with that of the Free Quakers who took up arms in the Revolutionary cause, thus swearing fealty and proving their loyalty to the rebellion.

The Arch Street Meeting House is a plain building living up to his and his client's principles, but Biddle spread his creative wings a bit, with the addition of Tuscan columns that highlight the entrances. Since his book delves into the then-fashionable Greek Revival style, it's clear had he lived longer he would have left a distinctive mark on the Philadelphia skyline.

The East Wing (men's meeting room) was built first in 1804 and holds displays related to the life of William Penn and the history of the Quaker faith in Philadelphia. The West Wing (women's meeting room) with its long wooden benches is decorated as it was when it opened in 1811. The floor and most of the windows, shutters, and hardware are original.

As a sign of its continuing importance, the Arch Street Meeting House still hosts the Philadelphia Yearly Meeting of the Religious Society of Friends.

Arch Street Friends Meeting House Information

Address: 320 Arch St.

Hours: 10 a.m. to 4 p.m. Mon through Sat; meetings for worship on Sun at 10:30 a.m. and Wed at 7 p.m. Visitors are always welcome to meetings for worship.

Admission: $2 donation is suggested. Meetings for worship are free.

Phone: (215) 627-2667

Website: archstreetfriends.org

Wheelchair accessibility: Ring bell at ramp in rear of building for access.

🔲 Side Trip: Benjamin Franklin Key Statue

Across from the Arch Street Meeting House look for the 9-foot-tall bronze bust of Benjamin Franklin staring serenely into the distance. The *Keys to Community* sculpture was installed in 2007 by artist James Peniston to replace the circa-1971 Penny Franklin statue that was deteriorating.

Look closely to see all the keys imprinted in the sculpture.

The artist went around to schools in the Philadelphia area to collect old keys from schoolchildren. Casts of the keys were impressed into the surface of the sculpture, which you can see when you get up close. In addition the students donated 1.8 million pennies ($18,000) to the project.

The statue sits next to the firehouse for Engine 8 of the Philadelphia Fire Department and also serves as a tribute to Philadelphia firefighters who have died in action, a fitting touch since Franklin organized the city's first firefighting brigade in 1736. Walk a few steps beyond the statue to check out a whimsical bronze relief of Franklin wearing a fire helmet that adorns the front of Engine 8's firehouse.

INDEPENDENCE MALL NORTH

This final segment of the Philadelphia Liberty Trail brings the revolutionary period of America to a close. It was such a volatile time that even the pacifist Quakers developed a splinter group willing to fight. Their **Free Quaker Meeting House** is located right on Independence Mall. Nearby pay respects at **Benjamin Franklin's grave** in **Christ Church Burial Ground,** along with the final resting places of four more signers of the Declaration of Independence.

As you emerge from the **National Constitution Center,** take a last look at Independence Hall standing majestically in front of you. Reflect on that steamy July almost 250 years ago, and the monumental

The final resting place for the greatest Philadelphian of all, Benjamin Franklin.

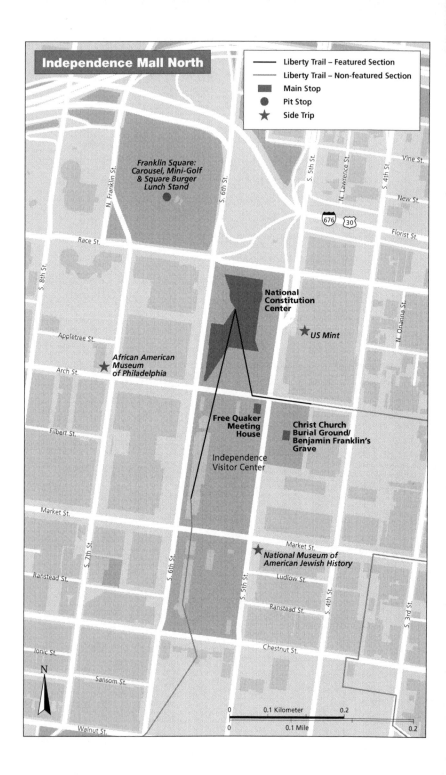

Independence Mall North

Liberty Trail – Featured Section
Liberty Trail – Non-featured Section
Main Stop
Pit Stop
Side Trip

Franklin Square:
Carousel, Mini-Golf
& Square Burger
Lunch Stand

N. Franklin St.

S. 6th St.

S. 5th St.

N. Lawrence St.

N. 4th St.

Vine St.

New St.

676 30

Florist St.

Race St.

S. 8th St.

National
Constitution
Center

N. Orianna St.

Appletree St.

US Mint

African American
Museum
of Philadelphia

Arch St.

Filbert St.

Free Quaker
Meeting
House

Christ Church
Burial Ground/
Benjamin Franklin's
Grave

Independence
Visitor Center

Market St.

S. 7th St.

S. 6th St.

S. 5th St.

Ranstead St.

Market St.

National Museum of
American Jewish History

Ludlow St.

S. 4th St.

Ranstead St.

S. 3rd St.

Ionic St.

Chestnut St.

N

Sansom St.

0   0.1 Kilometer   0.2

0   0.1 Mile   0.2

Walnut St.

events that took place within its solid brick walls that created a new nation.

Benjamin Franklin's Grave
Arch Street between 4th and 5th Streets

In 1790 Benjamin Franklin was laid to rest in the historic **Christ Church Burial Ground** alongside his wife, Deborah. As the constant foot traffic of visitors attests, his grave is one of the more popular sights in Philadelphia, ranking right up there with the Liberty Bell, Independence Hall, and the Rocky Steps.

Carl Van Doren, in his 1939 Pulitzer Prize–winning biography *Benjamin Franklin,* declared, "no other town, burying its great man, ever buried more of itself than Philadelphia with Franklin." It's clear that the spirit of Benjamin Franklin is found everywhere in Philadelphia.

The daily sweep of coins at Franklin's grave.

Visitors peer through an opening in the circa-1770 brick wall to view Franklin's grave, one of the most visited sites in Philadelphia.

The city now boasts the Franklin Institute, Benjamin Franklin Bridge, Benjamin Franklin Parkway, Franklin Square, Franklin Court, Franklin Field, Franklin Fountain, Benjamin Franklin Museum, Ben Franklin Technology Partners, and the Franklin Mills Mall; even the fan club for the local professional soccer team, the Philadelphia Union, is called the Sons of Ben. It's difficult to travel too many blocks in the city without coming across his legacy in one form or another.

In remembrance of one of Franklin's famous lines, "A penny saved is a penny earned," visitors now toss pennies onto his flat stone slab. Although perhaps a real tribute to Franklin's teachings would be saving them instead. Regardless, all that loose change goes to a good cause. The pennies (along with a few nickels, dimes, and quarters) are swept up daily and help maintain the grounds.

Here's the whimsical inscription that Franklin had written for his tombstone when he was a young printer:

THE BODY OF BENJAMIN FRANKLIN, PRINTER

Like the cover of an old book, Its contents torn out, And stript of its lettering and gilding,
Lies here, food for worms. But the work shall not be lost, For it will (as he believed) appear once more In a new and elegant edition,
Revised and corrected by The Author.

He certainly had a way with words, but Franklin ultimately changed his mind. The grave is simply marked: "Benjamin & Deborah Franklin 1790," as he instructed in his final will. Every year the Benjamin Franklin Birthday Celebration Committee celebrates Ben's birthday on the

---

And You Think Politics Is Rough Today

Those pining for civility in politics should have witnessed it in the rough-and-tumble days of America's early years. Historian George W. Boudreau in *Independence: A Guide to Historic Philadelphia* writes about a major snubbing that Benjamin Franklin received upon his death. Although he once owned slaves, in his later years Franklin joined the abolitionist movement and was the president of the **Pennsylvania Society for Promoting the Abolition of Slavery.** After Franklin died the House of Representatives officially went into mourning, but a similar move was blocked in the Senate by a group of pro-slavery southern senators who were irked by Franklin's late epiphany about human bondage. It's ironic that one of the most admired men in America and Europe did not receive universal acclaim by the politicians at home.

Friday closest to January 17. One of the highlights is a procession from the American Philosophical Society to Franklin's grave. See ushistory .org/celebration for information.

Benjamin Franklin's Grave Information

Location: Corner of 5th and Arch Streets

Hours: You can always view Franklin's grave through the wrought-iron fence. For the full experience, see the next section about visiting the Christ Church Burial Ground.

Admission: Free to view Franklin's grave from Arch Street. Coin tossing is optional, but hard to resist.

Phone: (215) 922-1695

Wheelchair accessibility: On a public sidewalk with wheelchair access

---

Christ Church Burial Ground
Arch Street between 4th and 5th Streets

The Christ Church Burial Ground is an impressive patch of American history. Purchased by **Christ Church** (see separate entry in the Old City section) in 1719, it now holds 1,400 stone markers in what was the far edge of colonial-era Philadelphia. The most famous Philadelphian of all, **Benjamin Franklin,** is buried here. (See prior section about viewing Benjamin Franklin's grave.)

Franklin is joined in eternal rest by four signers of the Declaration of Independence (the most signers of any burial ground anywhere): **Joseph Hewes, Francis Hopkinson, George Ross,** and **Dr. Benjamin Rush.** Rush is considered the "Father of American Psychiatry" due to his 1812 publication of *Medical Inquiries and Observations upon the Diseases of the Mind.*

Final resting place for five signers of the Declaration of Independence, including Benjamin Franklin.

Other prominent figures include: **Sarah Franklin Bache,** daughter of Benjamin and Deborah and a leader of the Ladies Association of Philadelphia, which helped raise funds for uniforms during the Revolutionary War; **John Dunlap,** printer of the broadside of the Declaration of Independence, which was read to the public for the first time on July 8, 1776; and **John Ross,** the first of Betsy Ross's three husbands.

Two men who owned homes on the Philadelphia Liberty Trail are also buried here: "Patriot Mayor" **Samuel Powel** along with his wife **Elizabeth,** and **Dr. Philip Syng Physick,** the Father of Modern Surgery. According to historian Jean K. Wolf, Dr. Physick had a fear of grave robbers. In his will "he requested that his body be left in a warm room to start to decay. Then it was to be put in a painted wooden coffin

Pirates of the Mediterranean . . . and Somali Coast
Interred at Christ Church Burial Ground is **US Navy Captain William Bainbridge.** During an illustrious career he was the captain of the 36-gun frigate USS *Philadelphia* in 1803 when it ran aground off Tripoli. He and his crew were captured by Tripolitan corsairs and held prisoner for 19 months. Bainbridge bounced back during the War of 1812 when he commanded USS *Constitution*, also known as Old Ironsides, in an epic victory over HMS *Java* off the coast of Brazil. Over the years several ships have been named after him. The most recent is the guided missile destroyer USS *Bainbridge,* which helped rescue the captain of the cargo ship *Maersk Alabama* from Somali pirates in 2009 (an incident dramatized in the 2013 movie *Captain Phillips).* One of the American sailors serving on board the *Bainbridge* during the rescue of Captain Phillips held his recent reenlistment ceremony here at the obelisk-shaped grave of the ship's namesake.

For an aerial view of Christ Church Burial Ground, request a room in the back at the Wyndham Hotel on 4th Street. For obvious reasons it's also quiet.

> **End of the Line**
>
> After George Washington, one of the most famous surveyors ever may be **Charles Mason,** who with Jeremiah Dixon created the **Mason-Dixon Line** that set the border between Pennsylvania and Maryland. **Mark Knopfler** even wrote a song called *Sailing to Philadelphia* about the event. After the completion of that project Mason, who was a renowned astronomer, returned to England where he worked at the Royal Observatory. But the lure of Philadelphia drew him back. He returned with his family in September 1786, penning a note to his friend Benjamin Franklin that he was working on a pet astronomy project. However, Mason died within a month of his arrival and the project that he was so excited about was lost for all time.
>
> Benjamin Franklin paid for Mason's burial, but did not add money for a headstone so the grave lay unmarked for over 200 years. Christ Church Burial Ground historian John Hopkins noted, "Charles Mason had a crater on the moon named after him, yet he had no earthly stone to remember his burial place." This oversight was corrected in 2013 when an authentic stone marker from the 1766 Mason-Dixon Line was placed in the ground to commemorate Mason. It was a fitting tribute for a man who spent so much of his life marking where things should be.

that would be placed in another of lead. A guard was to be assigned to his grave for six weeks." Apparently it worked and he remained undisturbed.

Physick's grandfather, **Philip Syng,** Philadelphia's answer to Paul Revere in the art of silversmithing, lies nearby. Syng crafted the inkstand that was used to sign the Declaration of Independence. The oldest headstone that has survived is of young Sarah Knowles who died in 1721, aged 11 months.

A noteworthy figure buried here is **David Salisbury Franks,** who was born in Philadelphia to a prominent Jewish merchant family. He moved up in rank in the Continental Army until he was the aide-de-camp to **Benedict Arnold** at the time the notorious traitor tried to hand the strategic fort at West Point over to the British. Although Franks was cleared of any complicity with Arnold's treachery,

Christ Church Burial Ground Information

Location: Arch Street, between 4th and 5th Streets

Hours: 10 a.m. to 4 p.m. Mon through Sat; noon to 4 p.m. Sun, Mar through Nov; noon to 4 p.m. Fri and Sat, Dec, weather permitting. Closed Jan and Feb, Easter Sunday, Thanksgiving, and Christmas.

Admission: Adults, $2; children, $1. It's worth purchasing the informational brochure and map available at the entry gate to get the most out of your visit. Guided tours are available throughout the day for an additional fee.

Phone: (215) 922-1695

Website: christchurchphila.org/Historic-Christ-Church/ Burial-Ground/59

Wheelchair accessibility: The main pathway is wheelchair accessible.

a cloud of suspicion hung over him that continued to shadow his career. He died penniless during the yellow fever epidemic that swept through Philadelphia in 1793. The quick thinking of a neighbor, who saw Franks's corpse piled on the coroner's wagon heading to a pauper's field, saved him from an anonymous burial.

Tour guides lead visitors around the burial ground and answer any questions. The tours are highly recommended to soak up the history of the people who are buried here.

Side Trip: United States Mint

The first mint authorized to produce a uniform American currency was established in Philadelphia in 1792. Up until then colonies printed their own money, presenting a hodgepodge of metal coins and paper money floating around, each with varying values that made it confusing for merchants selling goods and children buying penny candies.

The **Philadelphia Mint** is the largest coin manufacturing facility in the world and offers free self-guided tours. The informational brochure handed out with the tour will teach you everything you ever wanted to learn about making coins.

A hallway the length of a city block takes visitors 40 feet above the factory floor where millions of coins are manufactured each day. In fact, the mint can produce up to a million coins in just 30 minutes. That's a lot of pocket change. And how lucky are workers at the mint? Most people say they get a job to make money, but mint employees are literally *making money*.

Did you know that the force required to strike a nickel is equivalent to the combined bite strength of 157 great white sharks? If that doesn't sound scary, you certainly don't want to be a defective coin; they're sent to the ominous-sounding "condemned tanks" before being dumped in a waffling machine to be destroyed.

Visitors to the facility are subject to search by the United States Mint Police. Although that sounds like a squad unleashed by Willy Wonka to search for contraband peppermint candies, it's a serious job protecting the nation's money-making operations. You'll pass through airport-type security upon entering the building and adults will need to produce a photo ID.

United States Mint Information

Location: 151 N. Independence Mall East, bordering the east side of Independence Mall just across from the National Constitution Center

Hours: 9 a.m. to 4:30 p.m. Mon through Fri. Closed federal holidays except Memorial Day, July 4th, and Labor Day. Note: In a cost-saving move, production employees work 10-hour shifts from Mon through Thurs. If you visit on Friday you won't see much activity other than maintenance on machines.

Admission: Free

Phone: (215) 408-0112

Website: usmint.gov/about_the_mint/mint_facilities/index .cfm?action=PA_facilities

Wheelchair accessibility: The United States Mint is accessible for people with disabilities. Indicate any special needs upon arrival or in advance by calling (215) 408-0110.

Note: The United States Mint offers weekend and holiday hours during the summer; call ahead for summer tour information.

Free Quaker Meeting House
Southwest corner of 5th and Arch Streets

The Free Quaker Meeting House is unique on several levels: It's the only historic building still standing on Independence Mall proper and it's the oldest Quaker meeting house in Philadelphia, which is saying

By Quaker standards the new meeting house was pretty fancy.

something in a town also known as the Quaker City. It was built in 1783 by a group known as the Free, or Fighting, Quakers. Fighting Quakers? The Quakers were famously pacifists, so doesn't that sound like an oxymoron?

Tensions were rising in Philadelphia in 1776 as the clouds of war rumbled. Much of the populace was spouting words like "independence" and "freedom" and willing to raise their muskets to support such notions. The Pennsylvania Assembly required citizens to take a loyalty oath; this was a problem for Quakers who swore fealty to no government. (They'd pay the price for this perceived disloyalty. The next year 17 of them were evicted from Philadelphia and sent to Virginia.)

In this environment, with the colonies gearing up for war, how did a patriotic Quaker maintain his religious beliefs, yet still join the fight? After much debate about the issue, Quakers who were willing to support the Revolution formed a breakaway group known as the **Free Quakers.** They were founded in 1781 by Samuel Wetherill Jr. and his brother-in-law Timothy Matlack. If you've ever seen the Declaration of Independence at the National Archives in Washington you're familiar with Matlack's handwriting, since he likely transcribed the stirring document.

Starting in 1781, the newly formed Free Quakers recruited members and built their meeting house in 1783 and, as meeting houses go, it's relatively fancy. Note the architectural detailing that is more elaborate than traditional Quaker structures. The Flemish-bond brick pattern furnishes some style while the heavy brick pilasters on the corners were purely ornamental. In a sign that the authorities supported the new group, both George Washington and Benjamin Franklin contributed to the building fund.

Betsy Ross was a prominent member of the congregation. She'd been expelled from the Quakers years earlier when she married outside the faith to John Ross. Twice widowed, she remarried, this time to John Claypoole, and migrated to the Free Quakers, a sign of their greater tolerance than the mainstream Quakers. Eventually the two opposing groups of Quakers reconciled their differences and were reunited. By

1834 the building was no longer used for meetings and was rented out to tenants.

Although the meeting house is part of Independence National Historical Park, a separate group called **Historic Philadelphia** administers costumed reenactors who act the part of actual members of the congregation. Particularly entertaining is a character from the 1830s, **John Price Wetherill,** grandson of Samuel Wetherill who cofounded the Free Quakers. A druggist by profession, Wetherill opines on the latest fads in medicine, including cures for the scourge of flatulence. Women sought his assistance in making their eyes bright when young men were courting them; the practice of the day called for a drop of arsenic in each eye. It also led to blindness, so don't try that one at home.

Free Quaker Meeting House Information

Hours: Hours vary throughout the year but generally 11 a.m. to 4 p.m. daily, June 1 through Labor Day; 11 a.m. to 4 p.m. Sat and Sun the rest of the year.

Admission: Free

Phone: (215) 965-2305

Website: nps.gov/inde/free-quaker.htm

Wheelchair accessibility: All entrances and public spaces are wheelchair accessible.

Side Trip: National Museum of American Jewish History

Although this museum focuses on Jewish-American history, you don't have to be Jewish to appreciate it. It really conveys the universal experience of ethnic groups coming to America, while focusing on one slice of this immigration.

There were Jewish traders in the region before William Penn was awarded the land to start a colony. However, the first major wave of Jewish settlers, attracted by Penn's religious tolerance, arrived in Pennsylvania in the 1730s. On display is a wooden ark lintel carved with the Ten Commandments in Hebrew that was in the Lancaster home of Joseph Simon in 1750. The museum also highlights prominent Jewish figures in American history, such as **Haym Solomon,** who helped finance the American Revolution.

Visitors amble through a timeline of American history that follows Jewish settlers traveling west in Conestoga wagons. This room is hands on for children as they imagine what it was like to be uprooted with their family for such a risky move. Supplies are laid out and kids must decide which ones they should squeeze into the limited space on the wagon. A contrast to the pioneer experience is an exhibit on the growth of post–World War II suburbs such as Levittown.

National Museum of American Jewish History Information

Location: 100 S. Independence Mall East, bordering the east side of Independence Mall, at the southeast corner of 5th and Market Streets

Hours: 10 a.m. to 5 p.m. Tues through Fri; 10 a.m. to 5:30 p.m. Sat and Sun.

Admission: Adults, $12; seniors and youth (ages 13–21), $11; free to children 12 and under, members, and active military

Phone: (215) 923-3811

Website: nmajh.org

Wheelchair accessibility: Main entrance on Market Street and all public areas are wheelchair accessible.

Commodore Levy stands proudly outside Mikveh Israel synagogue.

Artifacts include Irving Berlin's piano and his manuscript of *God Bless America,* the royalties of which he donated to the Boy and Girl Scouts of America.

Across Market Street is the Mikveh Israel synagogue. The building opened on July 4, 1976, for the oldest Jewish congregation in Philadelphia and second oldest in the United States, dating to 1740. A statue out front commemorates the first Jewish US Navy Commodore, Uriah Philips Levy. An admirer of Thomas Jefferson, in 1836 he purchased the late president's estate at Monticello when it was in dilapidated condition and restored it to its former grandeur.

The **Mikveh Israel Cemetery,** which opened in 1740 on Spruce Street, is a separate side trip on the Washington Square and Society Hill section of the Philadelphia Liberty Trail.

National Constitution Center
525 Arch Street

> We the People of the United States, in Order to form a more perfect Union, establish Justice, insure domestic Tranquility, provide for the common defence, promote the general Welfare, and secure the Blessings of Liberty to ourselves and our Posterity, do ordain and establish this Constitution for the United States of America.
>
> —*Preamble to the United States Constitution*

The National Constitution Center celebrates the revolutionary ideas that were set forth in the US Constitution. With hindsight it appears that the creation of the United States and its emergence as a world power were foregone conclusions, but at its birth the nation's future was tenuous.

When the Continental Congress declared its independence from Great Britain in 1776 nothing was certain. There was still a war to win, and once that was settled there was a peace to sort out. When the war ended the 13 colonies were now 13 states and they were hardly united at all. They issued separate currencies, had their own militias, and were even scuffling over border disputes. From his perch at Mount Vernon, George Washington expressed his concern to James Madison that the young nation was "verging to anarchy and confusion!" The individual states could have descended into small independent countries forever riven with conflict. The Declaration of Independence may have set the colonies free from Great Britain, but it was the Constitution that drew them together as the United States.

The best place to start a visit is in the Kimmel Theater. This theater-in-the-round presents ***Freedom Rising,*** a 17-minute multimedia history of the Constitution presented by a live actor. He or she

Know your rights at the National Constitution Center.

starts out by boldly declaring the familiar words that begin the Constitution, "We the People," but follows it up with a question: "Who are we? What makes us a people?" The narrative continues with the colonies' struggle against Great Britain and the causes for seeking independence. As the actor continues, striking images from the American Revolution bombard the circular screen that surrounds the top of the theater.

The war was over, but now what? The states were "united" but perhaps only in name; they were operating as largely separate entities with their own political agendas. From this disarray emerged 55 delegates who gathered at the **Constitutional Convention** in Philadelphia in 1787, presided over by George Washington in the same room where the Declaration of Independence was signed, to create order out of chaos. The result of their efforts? The United States

Constitution, the document that formed the United States of America, created a framework of laws to govern it, and guaranteed certain rights for its citizens.

The presentation ends with rousing music and dramatic images from American history that leaves visitors inspired as the presenter ends with the challenge, "Now it is our decision—what will we do with our freedom?"

Visitors tour the museum after leaving the theater. It's set up in a circular fashion: The outer circle relates the history of constitutional issues such as voting rights while the inner one is more hands-on—you can vote in a mock election or pose for a photo taking the presidential oath of office.

Particularly compelling is a "tree" made up of 100 photos of American citizens, revealing how the search for freedom affected ordinary citizens. Included are **Mary Katherine Goddard,** a Baltimore publisher who printed the first copy of the Declaration of Independence with the names of all the signers in January 1777; **Robert Smalls,** a slave who commandeered a Confederate ship and delivered it to the Union fleet; and **Ileana Ros-Lehtinen,** the first Cuban-American and Hispanic woman elected to the House of Representatives.

Heavy Medal

The Liberty Medal is awarded annually by the National Constitution Center in Philadelphia to "men and women of courage and conviction who strive to secure the blessings of liberty to people around the globe." It was first awarded in 1988 to Lech Walesa. Other recipients include: Muhammad Ali, Jimmy Carter, Colin Powell, Bono, and a joint award in 1993 to Nelson Mandela and F. W. De Klerk for the struggle to end apartheid in South Africa. Six Liberty Medal winners have gone on to be awarded the Nobel Peace Prize.

For some exhibits you'll wish you had paid a bit more attention in your American history classes. A *Family Feud*-like setup lets visitors compete in a game of presidential trivia. You can also take a sample of the citizenship naturalization quiz. Afterwards watch a video of the

Shake hands with Benjamin Franklin in the Signers' Hall.

swearing-in ceremony for many of those who passed the quiz in real life. It's an emotional moment watching the newest Americans as they proudly display their citizenship papers to the camera.

The **Signers' Hall** contains life-sized bronze statues of 42 Founding Fathers, 39 of whom signed the Constitution and three who opposed the document. The latter group included George Mason and Edmund Randolph of Virginia and the mercurial Elbridge Gerry of Massachusetts, whose name lives on in today's political world in the serpentine congressional redistricting practice known as **gerrymandering.** Kids love wandering around this room, oohing and ahhing about George Washington's height, then comparing themselves to the diminutive James Madison. Judging from the well-worn patina on his outstretched hand, shaking hands with Benjamin Franklin is a popular activity too.

There are also rotating special exhibits. In the past they've ranged from the music of Bruce Springsteen to slavery at Thomas Jefferson's Monticello.

National Constitution Center Information

Hours: 9:30 a.m. to 5 p.m. Mon through Fri; 9:30 a.m. to 6 p.m. Sat, 12 p.m. to 5 p.m. Sun. Closed Thanksgiving, Christmas, and New Year's day.

Admission: Adults, $14.50; seniors and students, $13; children 4–12, $8; active military and children 3 and under, free

Phone: (215) 409-6700

Website: constitutioncenter.org

Wheelchair accessibility: All entrances and public spaces are wheelchair accessible.

Side Trip: African American Museum in Philadelphia

There are many stops along the Philadelphia Liberty Trail where African Americans—both free and enslaved—played a vital part. This museum presents an overview of the African-American experience in early Philadelphia.

The permanent exhibit, entitled "Audacious Freedom: African Americans in Philadelphia 1776–1876" chronicles the story with a massive interactive collage that allows visitors to select specific events and hear narrations related to them.

Young people in particular will enjoy the "Conversations" gallery, where life-sized video projections of prominent 18th-century Philadelphians such as **Absalom Jones, Richard Allen,** and **Frances Ellen Watkins Harper** "chat" with visitors about their lives and struggles.

The remainder of the museum is dedicated to rotating exhibits that highlight contemporary aspects of the African-American experience, whether political, cultural, or scientific. Recent examples include a photo essay on black farmers in America and a costume display of dresses from Diana Ross and the Supremes.

The **African American Museum in Philadelphia** is located at 701 Arch St. and is open Thurs to Sat 10 a.m. to 5 p.m., Sun noon to 5 p.m. Admission is $14 for adults, $10 for youths, students, and seniors. Children under 4 are free. Phone (215) 574-0380, aampmuseum.org.

Pit Stop: Franklin Square

Franklin Square is one of the original five squares that William Penn laid out in Philadelphia. It was named for Benjamin Franklin in 1825. One legend claims that he conducted his experiments with lightning nearby. That explains the silver *Bolt of Lightning* sculpture, designed by Isamu Noguchi, visible across North 6th Street from the square.

Take a spin on the carousel in Franklin Square.

Kids can burn off some energy at Philly mini-golf, a nifty miniature golf course that winds its way through dollhouse-like replicas of historic Philadelphia landmarks including Independence Hall, the Liberty Bell, and the Ben Franklin Bridge. If you'd rather spin around in circles than play a round, head across the square to the **Parx Liberty Carousel** where you can even ride a bald eagle.

Youngsters enjoy the Franklin Square playground. There are separate areas for older and younger kids along with some funky play equipment that looks like it was inspired by Salvador Dalí. It's one of the reasons Franklin Square has made several lists of top places for kids to run around and be, well, kids.

After working up an appetite, **Square Burger** is the perfect place to stop for burgers, hot dogs, or ice cream. It's a walk-up spot with outdoor seating. Their signature item is the Cake Shake, made up of a Tastykake

Butterscotch Krimpet (Philly's improved answer to the Twinkie) and caramel sauce blended with vanilla ice cream. It can be quite the sugar bomb so plan on sharing it with someone.

The Franklin Square playground is open year-round from 6 a.m. to 9 p.m. The carousel, mini-golf, and Square Burger are open seasonally from late March to Halloween. There are also clean public restrooms on the square. For up-to-date information on activities and opening hours of the attractions you can check online at historicphiladelphia.org/franklin-square/what-to-see or find them on Facebook: facebook.com/franklinsquarephiladelphia.

FARTHER AFIELD

Within both Philadelphia and the surrounding region there are several sights related to the early years of Pennsylvania and America that are also worth exploring.

Elsewhere in Philadelphia

Gloria Dei (Old Swede's) Church: Swedish immigrants set foot in the Delaware Valley in 1638 to create New Sweden, decades before William Penn was granted his colony. They built this church in 1700 to accommodate their growing numbers, making it the oldest church building in continuous use in Pennsylvania; it's reputedly the only building remaining in Philadelphia where William Penn set foot. It was also the setting for Betsy Ross's second marriage to Joseph Ashburn. Check out the colorful 17th-century wooden carvings of cherubs inside. Although it is part of the National Park Service, Gloria Dei is still an active church. Hours: Open daily. Service times: Sun at 10 a.m. (June, July, Aug); Sun at both 9 and 11 a.m. (Sept though May). Admission: Free. Columbus Boulevard and Christian Street, Philadelphia, PA 19147; (215) 389-1513; old-swedes.org.

Bartram's Garden: John Bartram was an 18th-century Quaker farmer whose "modest" goal was to catalog all the native plant life in North America, leading him to become America's premier botanist. Sited along the banks of the Schuylkill River, Bartram's plot of land was considered the first garden in America and attracted the likes of fellow farmers George Washington and Thomas Jefferson; seeds from the garden were even sold as far afield as London. Today the garden is a Philadelphia public park. Paid guided tours are available from early Apr through early Dec. Wetlands along the southern tip of the garden offer a prime viewing spot for redwing blackbirds and green herons and the wildflower-filled meadow offers a spectacular view of the Philadelphia skyline. Native plants are also available for purchase in the nursery. Hours: Dawn to dusk year-round; closed on Philadelphia city holidays. Admission: The gardens are free with guided tours extra; adults, $12; seniors and students, $10. Located at 54th Street and Lindbergh Boulevard, Philadelphia, PA 19143; (215) 729-5281; bartramsgarden.org.

The Woodlands: The 54-acre site is billed as a "one-of-a-kind 18th-century English pleasure garden, 19th-century rural cemetery, and a modern green oasis for its neighbors in bustling University City and West Philadelphia." The home at the center of this sylvan setting was rebuilt by William Hamilton in 1786 in the federal style; a distinguishing feature is the oval rooms, a precursor to the Oval Office at the White House. The home and grounds were also the inspiration for White Acre, the centerpiece of *Eat, Pray, Love* author Elizabeth Gilbert's novel *The Signature of All Things.* Hours: The grounds are open dawn to dusk year-round; mansion tours run every Wed, Apr thru Oct, from 10 a.m. until 2 p.m.; tours begin on the hour and last approximately 45 minutes. Admission: The grounds are free with mansion tours extra; adults, $10; seniors, $8. Located at 4000 Woodland Ave., Philadelphia, PA 19104; (215) 386-2181; woodlandsphila.org.

Eastern State Penitentiary: Go to prison on vacation? It's not so farfetched an idea. When novelist Charles Dickens took his grand tour of America in 1842 there were two must-see sights on his bucket list: Niagara Falls and Eastern State Penitentiary. The brooding Gothic pile was completed in 1829 and became the prototype for prisons worldwide. The innovative design by John Haviland features a central guard station with rows of individual cells radiating from it like spokes on a wheel. If you visit Philadelphia in October, it also hosts one of the eeriest haunted houses in America. Hours: 10 a.m. to 5 p.m. (last entry is 4 p.m.) daily; closed Thanksgiving Day, Christmas Eve, Christmas Day, and New Year's Day. Admission: adults, $14; seniors, $12; students,

$10. Located at 2027 Fairmount Ave., Philadelphia, PA 19130; (215) 236-3300; easternstate.org.

Historic Homes of Fairmount Park: It's hard to imagine now, but when these homes were built just on the other side of Center City, they were country retreats for those looking to escape the city's summer heat. Despite their proximity to the city, they still retain their bucolic settings, thanks to the creation of Fairmount Park. The seven estates represent one of the most important collections of 18th- and early 19th-century residential architecture in America. Among the highlights are: **Mount Pleasant,** which John Adams called "the most elegant seat in Pennsylvania"; the neoclassical **Lemon Hill,** boasting a commanding view of the Schuylkill River and Boathouse Row; and the antiques-filled **Woodford.** The Holiday Open House Tours when the homes are decorated for Christmas are quite popular. For information about visiting go to parkcharms.com.

Cliveden: The grand summer estate of colonial Chief Justice Benjamin Chew was completed in 1767. Ten years later it was almost destroyed when over 100 British troops barricaded themselves in Chew's house to stave off an American attack in the Battle of Germantown. Despite intense cannon and musket fire, the Americans only chipped away at the thick stone walls of Cliveden. Unable to dislodge the British, they retreated up Germantown Road into Montgomery County. The Chew family occupied the home for seven generations, right up until the 1950s; as a result much of the interior and furnishings are original. Hours: noon to 4 p.m. Thurs though Sun, Apr 1 through Dec 31; closed Jan through Mar, Thanksgiving Day, Christmas Eve, and Christmas. Admission: adults, $10; students, $6. Located at 6401 Germantown Ave., Philadelphia, PA 19144; (215) 848-1777; cliveden.org.

Germantown White House: Formerly called the **Deshler-Morris House,** the circa-1772 home was occupied by General Howe after the battle of Germantown in 1777. In 1793 it became a refuge for

President Washington when he fled the yellow fever epidemic. So yes, it is one place that can rightfully claim, "Washington slept here." In fact, he found the neighborhood so agreeable he returned with his family the following summer. It's now nicknamed the Germantown White House due to Washington's residency. Hours: 10 a.m. to 4 p.m. Fri, Sat, and Sun, Apr through Oct. Admission: free. Located at 5512 Germantown Ave., Philadelphia, PA 19144; (215) 965-2305; nps.gov/inde/history-culture/places-germantownwhitehouse.htm. *Note:* Due to federal budget cutbacks the Germantown White House is occasionally closed, so check first before visiting.

Fort Mifflin: Fort Mifflin flies under the radar, both literally and figuratively, in the Philadelphia region. Most locals are not aware of it due to its remote location, straddling the eastern edge of the main runways at Philadelphia International Airport. Eagle-eyed passengers who snagged a window seat get a bird's-eye view into the 21-sided structure. The fort played a key role during the American Revolution. After British General Howe occupied Philadelphia in September 1777, he couldn't supply his army via the Delaware River while American troops held the fort. They defied constant bombardment for over five weeks. During this time Washington's army slipped away to its eventual winter encampment at Valley Forge and lived to fight another day. Tours take visitors deep into the dark, damp interior of the fort where you'll learn about its use as a POW camp during the Civil War and why it's reputedly haunted. In addition to all that history, plane spotters will rarely find a better locale to watch jumbo jets thundering right overhead. Hours: 10 a.m. to 4 p.m. Mar 1 through mid-Dec, open by chance or appointment mid-Dec through Feb 28. Admission: adults, $6; students $3. Located at 4600 Hog Island Rd., Philadelphia, PA 19153; (215) 685-4167; fortmifflin.com.

Northeast of Philadelphia

Pennsbury Manor: A re-creation of the country estate that William Penn built in 1683. By 1767 the house was in a state of disrepair and the land was subdivided and sold. During the 1930s, the house was rebuilt in what was considered a "colonial" style at the time. It's not an authentic reproduction since there wasn't enough documentation to reveal the original home's floor plan and exact appearance. Today the 43-acre estate is a living history museum where costumed docents relate what life was like in colonial America. Rare furniture circa 1690 is on display. Hours: 9 a.m. to 5 p.m. Tues through Sat, Mar 1 through Dec 31; tours by appointment only from Jan 1 through Feb 28. Admission: adults $9; seniors $7; youth $5. Located at 400 Pennsbury Memorial Rd., Morrisville, PA 19067; (215) 946-0400; pennsburymanor.org.

Andalusia: Nicholas Biddle was a successful financier who oversaw the Second Bank of the United States. The earliest parts of his home overlooking the Delaware River were built in 1795. The impressive Greek Revival colonnaded portico, which would look right at home on the White House, was added in 1835. The interior is decorated with a valuable collection of late 18th- and 19th-century American, English, French, and Chinese furnishings used by generations of Biddles since the house was built. Hours: Mon to Fri 9 am to 3 pm; tours are by appointment only. Located at Biddle Lane, Bensalem, PA 19020; (215) 245-5479; andalusiapa.org.

Northwest of Philadelphia

Hope Lodge: Located on historic Bethlehem Pike, Hope Lodge is a grand example of early Georgian architecture that was built between 1743 and 1748 by Quaker merchant Samuel Morris. After their defeat at the Battle of Germantown, the Continental Army bivouacked here and in the surrounding hills for six weeks beginning in November 1777. The Army's surgeon general, Dr. John Cochran, occupied the mansion during this period. After a few skirmishes with British troops they moved on to Valley Forge. Henry Hope, after whose family the Hope diamond is named, purchased it for a relative in 1784. Modern heating and indoor plumbing were never installed in the main house, lending it an authentic period interior. Hours: Currently closed for tours due to state budget cutbacks but events are still being held on the grounds. Check website for updates. Located at 553 S. Bethlehem Pike, Fort Washington, PA 19034; (215) 646-1595; ushistory.org/hope.

Side Trip: Meetinghouse Antiques

If visiting all these historic homes has put you in the mood for acquiring some 18th- and early 19th-century American furniture and furnishings, stop by Meetinghouse Antiques at 509 Bethlehem Pike, in Fort Washington, about a quarter-mile north of Hope Lodge. Further information at boydsantiques.com.

Valley Forge National Historical Park: One of the most enduring images of the American Revolution is of ragtag American troops huddled in the snow during their harsh encampment at Valley Forge during the winter of 1777–78; while the soldiers were roughing it, the British army was nestled comfortably in occupied Philadelphia. But the American army took advantage of their winter hiatus. Under the tutelage of Prussian General Baron Von Steuben they were drilled into a formidable fighting force that was ready to take on the British come the spring campaign. The huts on display are reproductions, but the house that Washington used for his headquarters still stands. Visitors tread the very same halls where Washington contemplated the fate of his army and the young nation. With over 3,000 acres of rolling hills and woodland, the park is a wonderful place for hikes, bike rides, and picnics. Valley

Forge is located 20 miles west of Philadelphia. Hours: Visitor Center open 9 a.m. to 5 p.m. daily; summer hours are 9 a.m. to 6 p.m. daily. Closed Thanksgiving, Christmas, and New Year's Day. Park grounds open all year from 7 a.m. to dusk. Check website for operating hours of individual sites within the park. Located at 1400 N. Outer Line Dr., King of Prussia, PA 19406; (610) 783-1000; nps.gov/vafo.

Southwest of Philadelphia

Brandywine Battlefield: The Battle of the Brandywine was fought on September 11, 1777. Involving over 30,000 troops, it was the largest clash in the American Revolution. After a day of intense fighting, the Brits seized the momentum and the Americans retreated under cover of darkness, laying open the road to Philadelphia, which General Howe and his redcoats occupied two weeks later. The buildings that housed Washington and Lafayette are still standing, with Washington's headquarters open for tours. The 19-year-old Lafayette saw his first military action here and was wounded in the leg. Guided one-hour battlefield tours are available by appointment. The site is nestled in the heart of picturesque Chadds Ford, a region made famous in the paintings of Andrew Wyeth. Hours: Varies throughout the year so it's best to check the website for operating times and admission fees. Located at 491 Baltimore Pike, Chadds Ford, PA 19317; (610) 459-3342; brandywinebattlefield.org.

General Travel Information

Parking and Transportation

The Philadelphia Liberty Trail is a walking tour experience. If you arrive by plane, train, or bus, there is no need for a rental car. If you're driving into town, plan to park your car for the duration of your stay.

Parking

Parking is available in several structured and surface lots throughout the historic district, including a large lot underneath Independence Mall (entrances are on 5th and 6th Streets between Market and Arch Streets). Metered street parking is available in Old City, but many of these spaces have short time limits, particularly during daytime hours. Here are two websites that are helpful to find parking that have downloadable apps:

> philadelphia.bestparking.com: A comprehensive list of parking garages and lots, along with hourly, daily and overnight (where available) rates.

> parkme.com: A list of parking lots and garages, along with the ability to reserve a space at certain lots. This option comes in handy during busy travel times.

Trains

Amtrak: Philadelphia is a major stop in Amtrak's northeast corridor. Frequent trains arrive daily at the city's 30th Street Station, which is about a 10-minute taxi ride to the historic district.

Regional Rail Lines: Southeastern Pennsylvania Transportation Authority (SEPTA) operates a network of regional trains that extend throughout the Pennsylvania and Delaware suburbs, and up to Trenton, New Jersey. The Market East Station is approximately 4 blocks from Independence Mall. SEPTA offers "Independence Passes" (individual and family versions) that cover all transit travel on a single day for a reduced price, which can be purchased at the stations or ordered in advance by mail. For more information, visit septa.org/fares/pass/independence.html.

Visitors staying in southern New Jersey might consider the PATCO Speedline into Philadelphia, which has a stop at 8th and Market Streets, just 2 blocks from Independence Mall; ridepatco.org/

Airport Transportation

Philadelphia International Airport (PHL) is only 8 miles from central Philadelphia with easy access. Taxis charge a flat rate of approximately $30 for the 15- to 20-minute ride. A SEPTA train departs from each terminal every 30 minutes from about 5 a.m. to midnight; the ride to Market East Station takes 30 minutes. Check the PHL airport website for the latest fare information and train schedules: phl.org/passenger-info/transportationservices/pages/transport_default.aspx.

Buses

Traditional Bus Service: Offered through Greyhound and Trailways to the station at 10th and Filbert Streets (approximately 5 blocks from Independence Mall).

Point-to-point Service: Budget-minded travelers have a choice of carriers such as BoltBus and MegaBus offering direct routes from select northeastern cities. The Philadelphia stop for this service is near Amtrak's 30th Street Station. For more information and apps go to: us.megabus.com/Default.aspx or boltbus.com/Default.aspx.

Tours

Whether you're seeking a quick overview of the historic district or want to delve deeper into a specific topic, there are a wide variety of tours to suit all interests. (*Note:* a few tours and programs associated with the National Park Service are free; these are noted below.)

Daytime Walking Tours

Audio Walk and Tour (800-537-7676; phlvisitorcenter.com): Sightsee through the historic district on your own time. Tour includes rental of an MP3 player and a detailed map highlighting over 20 important historic sites including Independence Hall and the Liberty Bell.

The Constitutional Walking Tour (215-525-1776; theconstitutional .com): A 75-minute, 1.25-mile walking tour covering over 20 sites in the historic district gives a good overview. Tours depart from the Constitution Center.

The Constitutional Self-Guided Audio Tour (215-525-1776; theconstitutional.com): Those interested in exploring at their own pace can purchase an audio version of the Constitutional tour and download it to a personal MP3 player.

Franklin's Footsteps Walking Tour (215-389-8687; phillytour .com/products-tours.php): Tour of the historic district encompassing sights in and near Independence National Historical Park, including Ben Franklin's grave, the Liberty Bell, and others. The 75-minute tour departs from the Independence Visitor Center.

National Park Service Tours (Free; 800-537-7676, nps.gov/inde/ special-programs.htm): Park rangers lead tours and presentations on specialty topics throughout Independence Park. Tours and presentations vary by season; check the website or the Visitor Center for updated information.

Once Upon a Nation: Historic Reenactments (Free; 215-629-4026; historicphiladelphia.org): A muster of the Continental Army, a chat with Betsy Ross, and a public reading of the Declaration of Independence are a few of the ways this group brings history to life. Check the website for a complete list of events and times.

Once Upon a Nation: Storytelling Benches (Free; 215-629-4026; historicphiladelphia.org): Scattered throughout Independence Park and its surroundings are 10 semicircular benches where uniformed storytellers relate tales of Revolutionary days. Check the website for a map of bench locations and storytelling times.

Philadelphia Urban Adventures (215-280-3746; philadelphiaurban adventures.com): Group walking tours that incorporate stops at a local coffee shop and brewpub into the 2-hour itinerary around Independence Park and environs.

Preservation Alliance of Greater Philadelphia Architectural Walking Tours (215-546-1146; preservationalliance.com/ events/architectural-walking-tours): This nonprofit group leads 90- to 120-minute tours covering a variety of themed architectural tours, such as historic churches, banks, or homes. Guided tours are offered from May through Oct and vary by date; check the website for the current schedule.

Evening Walking Tours

Ghost Tours of Philadelphia (215-413-1997; ghosttour.com): Tours throughout the historic district, by foot or by trolley, that explore some of the spookier aspects of Philadelphia's past.

Grim Philly Twilight Tours (856-829-3100; grimphilly.com): If your historic interests tend toward the macabre, join college professor Joe Wojie on one of his nine adult-themed jaunts that tell tales of colonial hangings, pirates, and other creepy mayhem on the cobblestone streets.

Independence After Hours (215-525-1776; historicphiladelphia .org): Begin your evening with a colonial repast at City Tavern, followed by a special candlelit visit to Independence Hall, where you witness a reenactment of the debates that went on within these historic walls.

Spirits of '76 Ghost Tour (215-525-1776; spiritsof76.com): Described as "one part history, two parts haunt," this 75-minute walking tour invokes the memories of heroes and villains of the Revolutionary era.

Twilight Tours (Free; 215-861-4971; friendsofindependence.org): This nonprofit group guides visitors on a walk through Independence Park to view the historic building exteriors as they come aglow in the evening. Mid-June through Labor Day, departing from the Visitor Center.

Wheels and Hooves

Awfully Nice Tours (215-923-8516; awfullynicetours.com): A company that offers full- and half-day private driving tours with a variety of historic itineraries in Philadelphia and the surrounding environs.

Horse-Drawn Carriages (215-923-8516; phillytour.com): Clip-clop in an open carriage for up to six people as guides regale you with interesting tidbits on historic streets. Daytime drives are 15, 30, or 60 minutes, tickets are available online or at the Visitor Center. (*Note:* Evening rides are available by reservation.)

Philly by Segway (877-331-6197; philadelphiabysegway.com): Glide along on a 4-mile, 1-hour tour through the historic district and South Philly, including a stop at the Italian Market.

Philadelphia Segway Tours by Wheel Fun (805-650-7770; phila delphia.segwaytoursbywheelfun.com): This 90-minute tour rolls by over 20 sights in the historic district. Tours depart from the Visitor Center.

Travel Resources

These websites will help you plan your visit to Philadelphia. They are listed along with some activities that will get you into the colonial spirit. A few of the sites have downloadable apps for smartphones.

General Visitor Information

Visit Philly (visitphilly.com): The official website of Visit Philadelphia, the city's tourism organization. Details about attractions, events, hotels, restaurants, and more.

Discover PHL (discoverphl.com): The official website of the Philadelphia Convention and Visitors Bureau, focusing on information for international visitors and conventions.

Independence National Historical Park (nps.gov/inde): The National Park Service's main site for all things related to Independence National Historical Park. The Park also offers a cool app for smartphones and tablets that includes maps, audio tours, and photos that you can download from the website.

Philadelphia Visitor Center (phlvisitorcenter.com): Located right on Independence Mall, the center for all visitor-related activity in Independence Park, as well as other tours and events in the historic district.

Visit Pennsylvania (visitpa.com): Official tourism website of the state of Pennsylvania, which has useful information about the Philadelphia environs, as well as other destinations in the state.

Local Events and Activities

Old City District (oldcitydistrict.org): Up-to-the-minute guide of activities in the neighborhood around Christ Church, Franklin Court, and the Betsy Ross House.

Philly Fun Guide (phillyfunguide.com): Provides a calendar of regional art, entertainment, and sporting events.

South Street Headhouse District (southstreet.com): Current information about happenings in and around Headhouse Square and Society Hill, including Headhouse Market.

Uwishunu (uwishunu.com): Official blog of VisitPhilly, this site (pronounced "you wish you knew") provides updated information about ongoing events in and around the city.

Historic and Background Information

The Encyclopedia of Greater Philadelphia (philadelphiaencyclopedia.org): Comprehensive collection of essays and articles about Philadelphia history and culture, written by many of the city's best-known writers and scholars, including at least one Pulitzer Prize winner.

USHistory.org (ushistory.org): Sponsored by the not-for-profit Independence Hall Association, this comprehensive site specializes in colonial and Revolutionary history with a focus on Philadelphia.

Fun Stuff for Kids
(and Adults Who Act Like Kids)

Charters of Freedom (archives.gov/exhibits/charters/declaration_sign.html): Nifty website where you can sign the Declaration of Independence in colonial script and print it out with your name added to the 56 signers.

USHistory.org (ushistory.org/betsy/flagstar.html): Learn how to make a five-pointed star with a single cut, just like the ones Betsy Ross used on her early flags.

National Treasure: The movie starring Nicolas Cage rekindled interest in early American history among young people. Much of it was filmed at stops on the Philadelphia Liberty Trail. It's worth viewing before arriving in Philadelphia.

Where to Stay

The best way to immerse yourself in the Philadelphia Liberty Trail is by staying overnight in the historic area. There is something magical about walking by Independence Hall and the other stately buildings in the quiet of the evening when soft lights cast an enchanting glow on their timeless brick exteriors. There are also many unique restaurants nearby (see separate **Where to Eat** section).

There are several hotels in different price ranges in the historic district. A few options are near the Pennsylvania Convention Center several blocks away.

Note: Some hotels in the suburbs list themselves as "Philadelphia-West" or "Historic Philadelphia Region" or something similar, seeking to highlight their proximity to the historic sights. These suburban locations will likely be cheaper, although less convenient. Be sure to confirm the location if you choose this option; some hotels are near public transportation, making car-free access to the city easier.

Hotels Along or Near the Philadelphia Liberty Trail

Apple Hostels (32 Bank St.; 215-922-0222; applehostels.com): A budget option for the backpacker crowd, it offers dormitory-style accommodations, and 2 private rooms, for about 60 guests, all with communal bathrooms, kitchen, and free Wi-Fi. The location is quite central, a narrow side street near Carpenters' Hall.

Holiday Inn Express Philadelphia—Penn's Landing (100 N. Columbus Blvd.; 215-627-7900; hiepennslanding.com): Formerly the Comfort Inn, this 184-room property is wedged into a slice of land between I-95 and Columbus Boulevard. The rooms were recently renovated; request one facing east toward the Delaware River to avoid highway noise. Free breakfast and Wi-Fi.

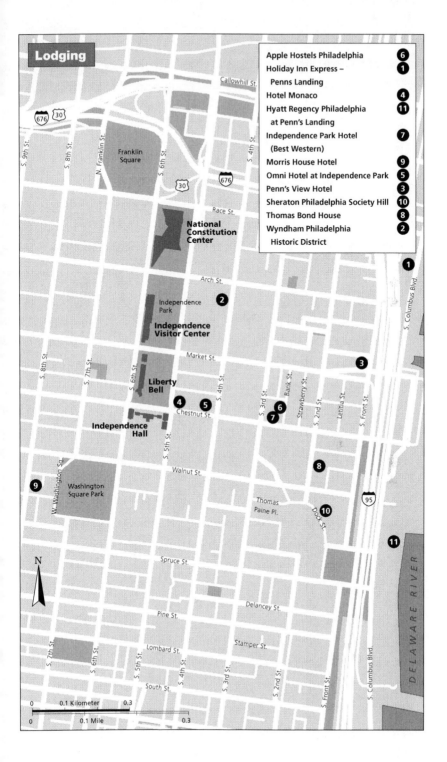

Lodging

Hotel	#
Apple Hostels Philadelphia	6
Holiday Inn Express – Penns Landing	1
Hotel Monaco	4
Hyatt Regency Philadelphia at Penn's Landing	11
Independence Park Hotel (Best Western)	7
Morris House Hotel	9
Omni Hotel at Independence Park	5
Penn's View Hotel	3
Sheraton Philadelphia Society Hill	10
Thomas Bond House	8
Wyndham Philadelphia Historic District	2

Hotel Monaco (433 Chestnut St.; 215-925-2111; monaco-philadelphia.com): This hip, funky outpost of the Kimpton chain boasts a premier location in a renovated 1920s bank building overlooking Independence Hall. The 286-room hotel has a popular rooftop bar and liberal pet-friendly policy. Wi-Fi is free for members of the hotel loyalty program.

Hyatt Regency Philadelphia at Penn's Landing (201 S. Columbus Blvd.; 215-928-1234; pennslanding.hyatt.com): Philadelphia's only hotel on the Delaware River waterfront, this high rise property with 384 rooms is across I-95 from Society Hill. Rooms offer views of the water or city skyline. An indoor pool with a river view is popular with kids.

Independence Park Hotel (Best Western PLUS) (235 Chestnut St.; 215-922-4443; independenceparkhotel.com): A small (36-room) property in a central location near Carpenters' Hall. Most rooms face an interior atrium; Chestnut Street rooms are brighter, but might be noisier. Breakfast and Wi-Fi included in rates.

Morris House Hotel (225 S. 8th St.; 215-922-2446; morrishousehotel.com): This elegant boutique hotel with only 15 rooms and suites is located in a colonial-era mansion just off Washington Square. Room rates include Wi-Fi, breakfast, and afternoon tea. The restaurant's garden is popular for wedding receptions.

Omni Hotel at Independence Park (401 Chestnut St.; 215-925-0000; omnihotels.com): Only 1 block from Independence Hall, most of this hotel's 150 rooms and suites overlook leafy Independence Park and the Second Bank of the United States. Wi-Fi is free for Omni loyalty members.

Penn's View Hotel (Front and Market Streets; 215-922-7600; pennsviewhotel.com): Boutique hotel comprised of several former town-houses with 51 rooms and suites. Rooms facing Front Street boast spectacular views of the river and Ben Franklin Bridge; however, they also overlook I-95. Light sleepers might prefer the less scenic, but quieter, rooms at the back. Some rooms have fireplaces; breakfast and Wi-Fi are included. Official address is 14 N. Front St. but GPS may send you in the wrong direction.

Sheraton Philadelphia Society Hill (1 Dock St.; 215-238-6000; sheratonphiladelphiasocietyhill.com): A 364-room property that feels more intimate, this full-service hotel is nestled at the edge of Society Hill on picturesque Dock Street. Completely renovated in 2013, its chic decor blends with traditional touches, including ultra-comfy beds with luxury linens. The lobby's cyber cafe is a popular spot to surf the net with a cup of joe, while the indoor pool keeps kids happy. Free treats such as authentic Philly soft pretzels with mustard are offered in the afternoon.

Thomas Bond House (129 S. 2nd St.; 215-923-8523; thomasbond housebandb.com): Overlooking the open square of Welcome Park, this B&B offers a traditional experience in a 1769 townhouse. Some of the 12 rooms have a working fireplace; breakfast and Wi-Fi are included. *Note:* no children 10 or under.

Wyndham Philadelphia Historic District (400 Arch St.; 215-923-8660; phillydowntownhotel.com): This full-service hotel got a head-to-toe makeover in 2014 when it upgraded from the Holiday Inn to Wyndham brand. Rooms are understated modern, with comfortable beds and fast free Wi-Fi. Only 1 block from Independence Mall, the hotel is tucked in between the Arch Street Friends' Meeting House and Christ Church Burial Ground, offering a quiet setting with historic views out front or back. The outdoor rooftop pool affords vistas of Old City.

Hotels near the Pennsylvania Convention Center

Courtyard Philadelphia Downtown (21 N. Juniper St.; 215-496-3200; marriott.com): Housed in a 1920s building, this 491-room property in the Marriott family offers rooms with 11-foot ceilings and free Wi-Fi. Some rooms have views of City Hall.

Home2Suites by Hilton Philadelphia-Convention Center (1200 Arch St.; 215-627-1850; home2suites3.hilton.com/en/index

.html): All accommodations in this 248-room property are suites with full kitchens. Rates include complimentary Wi-Fi and breakfast. Directly opposite the Convention Center and Reading Terminal Market. *Note:* Entrance is at 75 N. 12th St.

Loews Philadelphia Hotel (1200 Market St.; 215-627-1200; loews hotels.com) The international style of this former office building was ahead of its time when it opened in 1932. It's now a 581-room hotel with sleek design, skyline views from the higher floors, free Wi-Fi in guest rooms, and special amenities for pets.

Philadelphia Marriott Downtown (1201 Market St.; 215-625-2900; marriott.com) The city's largest full-service hotel offers 1,400 rooms and is adjacent to the Pennsylvania Convention Center and Reading Terminal Market.

Where to Eat

After a day exploring the Philadelphia Liberty Trail, let your taste buds do some exploring of their own. Philadelphia offers a cornucopia of dining choices; those listed below are all located in the historic district. Check with each restaurant directly for specific opening days and times.

Legend:

B: Breakfast
L: Lunch
D: Dinner
Br: Brunch (usually weekends)
Late: Limited menu after 10 p.m.
⬛ : Child-friendly and/or children's menu
Continuous: The restaurant does not close between mealtimes, although the menu may switch over at some point from breakfast to lunch to dinner to late. These spots come in handy on those days when you want a meal during an in-between time (or you're trying to feed the kids before a place gets too crowded).

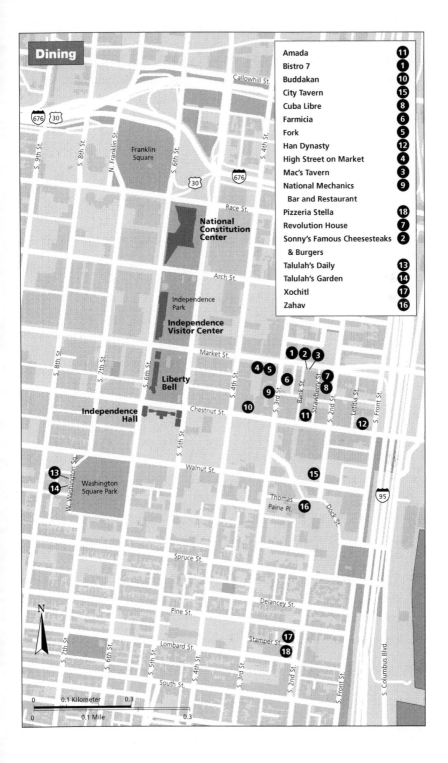

Dining

Amada	11
Bistro 7	1
Buddakan	10
City Tavern	15
Cuba Libre	8
Farmicia	6
Fork	5
Han Dynasty	12
High Street on Market	4
Mac's Tavern	3
National Mechanics Bar and Restaurant	9
Pizzeria Stella	18
Revolution House	7
Sonny's Famous Cheesesteaks & Burgers	2
Talulah's Daily	13
Talulah's Garden	14
Xochitl	17
Zahav	16

Amada (217 Chestnut St.; 215-625-2450; amadarestaurant.com): The first of Iron Chef winner Jose Garces's restaurants, this popular spot serves up stylish Spanish tapas and entrees. Meals: L, D, Br

Bistro 7 (7 N. 3rd St., 215-931-1560, bistro7restaurant.com): A modern French bistro with only a few tables, serving delectable entrees you'd be unlikely to make at home. BYOB. Meals: D

Buddakan (325 Chestnut St.; 215-574-9440; buddakan.com): Contemporary pan-Asian cuisine served in a chic, swanky atmosphere. Meals: L, D

City Tavern (138 S. 2nd St.; 215-413-1443; citytavern.com): Excellently prepared colonial-inspired fare served in a historic setting. For a more complete description, see the Pit Stop listing in the Carpenters' Court chapter. Meals: L–D (continuous)

Cuba Libre (10 S. 2nd. St.; 215-627-0666; cubalibrerestaurant.com) Take a mini-trip to the forbidden island of Cuba in an evocative "indoor street" setting. Latin floor show late nights on weekends. Meals: L, D, Br

Farmicia (15 S. 3rd. St.; 215-627-6274; farmiciarestaurant.com): Fresh, New American farm-to-table cuisine. Meals: B weekends, L, D, Br

Fork (306 Market St.; 215-625-9425; forkrestaurant.com) Elegant New American cuisine served in an equally sophisticated dining room. Meals: L, D, Br

Han Dynasty (123 Chestnut St., 215-922-1888, handynasty.net): Fresh, clever Chinese food where you order dishes on a spiciness scale of 1 to 10. Unless your tongue loves 5-alarm chili, stick to "heat" numbers below 5. Meals: L–D–Late (continuous)

High Street on Market (308 Market St.; 215-625-0988; highstreetonmarket.com): More casual sister restaurant to Fork, offering innovative comfort food of the highest quality along with some delicious skip-the-diet baked goods. Meals: B–L (continuous), D

Mac's Tavern (226 Market St.; 267-324-5507; macstavern.com): Traditional, no-nonsense tavern atmosphere with excellent gastropub food. Decor reflects a TV connection: Two of the owners star in the series *It's Always Sunny in Philadelphia*. Meals: L–D–Late (continuous)

National Mechanics Bar and Restaurant (22 S. 3rd St.; 215-701-4883; nationalmechanics.com): Traditional pub grub and comfort food served in a cool old bank setting. For more information see the Pit Stop in the Carpenters' Court section. Meals: L, D–Late (continuous), Br

Pizzeria Stella (2nd and Lombard Sts.; 215-320-8000; pizzeria stella.net): Brick oven pies of both the traditional and funky variety (like truffles and eggs), along with appetizers and salads in a bustling Headhouse Square setting. Meals: L–D (continuous)

Revolution House (200 Market St., 215-625-4566, revolution house.com): Upscale pizza, sandwiches, and salads in a friendly atmosphere, with a second-story dining room and rooftop terrace providing sweeping views of Christ Church. Meals: L–D (continuous), Br

Sonny's Famous Cheesesteaks & Burgers (228 Market St.; 215-629-5760; sonnyscheesesteaks.com): When in Philly, you have to try at least one cheesesteak. For more info (including a primer on cheesesteak lingo) see the Pit Stop in the Old City Chapter. Meals: L–D–Late (continuous)

Talula's Daily (208 W. Washington Sq.; 215-592-6555; talulasdaily .com): In addition to daytime casual fare (see Pit Stop in the Washington Square chapter), this friendly spot offers a nightly "supper" showcasing local ingredients with a single fixed-price menu that changes monthly; seating is at individual and communal tables. Meals: B–L (continuous), D

Talula's Garden (210 W. Washington Square; 215-592-7787; talulas garden.com): Chef/co-owner Aimee Olexy's more upscale offering, cooking up innovative farm-to-table fare in an urbane "city garden"

setting. Olexy is a cheese expert; try one of her signature sampler plates for a novel dessert option. Meals: D, Br

Xochitl (408 S. 2nd St.; 215-238-7280; xochitlphilly.com): Refined "Nuevo Mexicano" in a sleek setting on charming Headhouse Square. A selection of ceviches, entrees, and creative tacos make up the menu. Meals: D

Zahav (237 St. James Pl.; 215-625-8800; zahavrestaurant.com): An ultra-classy take on Israeli street-food fare, stressing freshness and unique combinations. Most menu items are either small plates or designed to share, such as the five different varieties of freshly made hummus. Meals: D

When Life Gives You Lemons . . .

. . . make lemon meringue pie. Early Philadelphians enjoyed the desserts of Mrs. Goodfellow, a culinary pioneer (and an ancestor of Jacqueline Bouvier Kennedy Onassis) who owned a bakery and cooking school on Dock Street. She is credited with developing this elegant dessert, which was all the rage in the early 1800s.

Mrs. Goodfellow's pie is made with lots of eggs, butter, and fresh lemons, topped with a fluffy caramelized meringue that is the perfect complement to the rich custard beneath.

Chef Walter Staib at City Tavern serves this authentic version for dessert. It's a slice of tart and tasty history.

Mrs. Goodfellow's Lemon Meringue Pie

3 large eggs
7 large egg yolks
1 cup granulated sugar, divided
Zest of 2 lemons
1 cup freshly squeezed lemon juice
8 ounces (2 sticks) cold unsalted butter, cubed
1 recipe Pâte Brisée (recipe below), in a 9-inch pie pan, baked and cooled
5 large egg whites

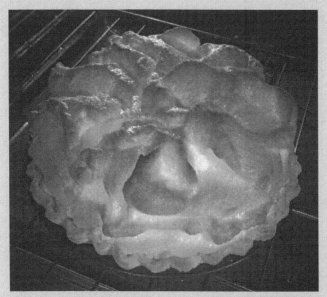

Definitely try this at home. Our rendition of Mrs. Goodfellow's Lemon Meringue Pie.

In a stainless steel saucepot, whisk together the eggs, egg yolks, ¾ cup of the sugar, and the lemon zest until combined.

Whisk in the lemon juice and cook over medium heat, stirring constantly, until the custard is very thick. When you drag a spatula through it, you should see the bottom of the pot for a few seconds before the curd falls back on itself.

Remove from the heat, pour the curd into a large bowl, and whisk in the butter.

Let stand, stirring occasionally, until the curd cools slightly.

Pour the curd into the pie shell, cover with plastic wrap, and chill until the curd is cold.

Preheat the oven to 400°F.

In the clean, dry bowl of an electric mixer, whip the egg whites on medium speed until foamy. Sprinkle in the remaining ¼ cup of sugar, 1 tablespoon at a time, and whip on high speed until stiff, glossy peaks form.

Spoon or pipe the meringue over the cooled curd and bake until the meringue has browned, about 12 to 15 minutes. Serve at room temperature.

Chef's Note: Low heat and constant stirring are imperative when making curd in order to prevent scrambling the eggs and/or burning the curd.

Pâte Brisée (Pie Crust)

1⅔ cups sifted all-purpose flour

¼ teaspoon salt

4 ounces (1 stick) cold unsalted butter, cubed

4–5 tablespoons ice water

In a medium-sized bowl, stir together flour and salt.

Using a pastry cutter, or your hands, cut in the cold butter until the mixture is a coarse crumble.

Sprinkle in water 1 tablespoon at a time and toss together until a dough ball starts to form. Add only enough water to hold the ball together.

Form the dough into a disc, wrap tightly in plastic wrap, and refrigerate for at least 30 minutes before use.

When ready to use, preheat an oven to 400°F.

Roll out the dough on a floured surface into a round about ¼ inch thick and place into pie pan.

To prebake for lemon meringue pie, line the pie dough with aluminum foil or parchment paper and gently pour in dried beans or rice to weigh down the dough and prevent it from buckling in the pan. Bake 15 minutes, or until golden brown.

Originally published in *A Sweet Taste of History: More than 100 Elegant Dessert Recipes from America's Earliest Days* by Chef Walter Staib.

Suggested Reading

Adams, John and Charles Francis Adams. *Letters of John Adams, Addressed to His Wife.* Charles C. Little and James Brown, Boston, MA: 1841.

Beeman, Richard. *Plain, Honest Men: The Making of the American Constitution.* Random House, New York, NY: 2009.

Beeman, Richard. *Our Lives, Our Fortunes & Our Sacred Honor: The Forging of American Independence, 1774–1776.* Basic Books, New York, NY: 2013.

Boudreau, George W. *Independence: A Guide to Historic Philadelphia.* Westholme Publishing, Yardley, PA: 2012.

Chidsey, Donald Barr. *July 4, 1776: The Dramatic Story of the First Four Days of July, 1776.* Crown Publishers, New York, NY: 1958.

Cotter, John L., Michael Parrington, and Daniel G. Roberts. *The Buried Past: An Archaeological History of Philadelphia.* University of Pennsylvania Press, Philadelphia, PA: 1992.

Cousins, Frank and Phil Madison. *The Colonial Architecture of Philadelphia.* Little, Brown and Company, Boston, MA: 1920.

Diamond, Becky. *Mrs. Goodfellow: The Story of America's First Cooking School.* Westholme Publishing, Yardley, PA: 2012.

Dorr, Benjamin. *A Historical Account of Christ Church, Philadelphia, From Its Foundation, A.D. 1695, to A.D. 1841.* Swords, Stanford and Co., New York, NY: 1841.

Drinker, Elizabeth Sandwith. *Extracts from the Journal of Elizabeth Drinker, from 1759 to 1807, A.D.* Edited by Henry D. Biddle. J. B. Lippincott Company, Philadelphia, PA: 1889.

Ellis, Joseph J. *American Creation: Triumphs and Tragedies at the Founding of the Republic.* Alfred A. Knopf, New York, NY: 2007.

Franklin, Benjamin. *The Autobiography of Benjamin Franklin.* American Book Company, New York, NY: 1896.

Huntington, Tom. *Ben Franklin's Philadelphia: A Guide.* Stackpole Books, Mechanicsburg, PA: 2006.

Lyons, Jonathan. *The Society for Useful Knowledge: How Benjamin Franklin and Friends Brought the Enlightenment to America.* Bloomsbury Press, New York, NY: 2013.

Madison, Dolley and Lucia Beverly Cutts. *Memoirs and Letters of Dolley Madison.* Houghton, Mifflin & Company, Boston, MA: 1886.

Miller, Marla R. *Betsy Ross and the Making of America.* Henry Holt and Company, New York, NY: 2010.

Mires, Charlene. *Independence Hall in American Memory.* University of Pennsylvania Press, Philadelphia, PA: 2002.

Staib, Chef Walter. *A Sweet Taste of History: More than 100 Elegant Dessert Recipes from America's Earliest Days.* Lyons Press, Guilford, CT: 2013.

Tatum, George B. *Philadelphia Georgian: The City House of Samuel Powel and Some of Its 18th Century Neighbors.* Wesleyan, Indianapolis, IN: 1976.

Thomas, George, et al. *Buildings of Pennsylvania: Philadelphia and Eastern Pennsylvania.* University of Virginia Press, Charlottesville, VA: 2010.

Unger, Harlow Giles. *America's Second Revolution: How George Washington Defeated Patrick Henry and Saved a Nation.* John Wiley & Sons, Hoboken, NJ: 2007.

Weigley, Russell F., Editor. *Philadelphia: A 300-Year History*. W.W. Norton & Company, New York, NY: 1982.

Westcott, Thompson. *The Historic Mansions and Buildings of Philadelphia, With Some Notice of Their Owners and Occupants*. L. H. Everts & Company, Philadelphia, PA: 1884.

Books to Inspire Young Historians

Andersen, Laurie Halse. *Fever 1793*. Simon and Schuster, New York, NY: 2002.

Avi. *The Fighting Ground*. Harper Collins, New York, NY: 1984.

Cohn, Scotti. *Liberty's Children: Stories of Eleven Revolutionary War Children*. Globe Pequot Press, Guilford, CT: 2004.

Gutman, Dan. *Back in Time with Benjamin Franklin: A Qwerty Stevens Adventure*. Simon and Schuster, New York, NY: 2005.

Kallen, Stuart A. *Life During the American Revolution*. Lucent Books, San Diego, CA: 2002.

Lloyd, Sandra Mackenzie (Ed.). *Patriots, Pirates, Heroes and Spies: Stories from Historic Philadelphia*. Historic Philadelphia, Inc., Philadelphia, PA: 2008.

Noble, Trinka Hakes. *The Scarlet Stockings Spy*. Sleeping Bear Press, Ann Arbor, MI: 2004.

Roop, Peter, Connie Roop, and Zachary Trover. *The Secret Adventure of John Darragh, Revolutionary Spy*. Graphic Universe, Minneapolis, MN: 2010.

Sanders, Nancy L. *America's Black Founders: Revolutionary Heroes and Early Leaders*. Chicago Review Press, Chicago, IL: 2010

Zeinert, Karen. *Those Remarkable Women of the American Revolution*. The Millbrook Press, Brookfield, CT: 1996.

Index

Made in the USA
Middletown, DE
03 December 2019